Yorkshire LAUGHTER

by Maurice Colbeck
Illustrated by Albin Trowski

'A wealth of traditional northern humour'
WHITBY GAZETTE

'A calculated insult'
LANCASHIRE LIFE

The Whitethorn Press Limited

DEDICATED
to the folk living West of the Pennines in
the confident assumption
that they will always take a
Yorkshireman's joke . . .
And very likely pass it off as their own.

First published in 1978
Reprinted 1979
Second Reprint 1981
© The Whitethorn Press Limited
Thomson House
Withy Grove
Manchester M60 4BL
England
ISBN 0 9506055 1 4

Litho Preparation by
Lapex Printing Limited
Heswall, Wirral.
Printed by
Carrprint Ltd.,
Barnoldswick.

THE AUTHOR

Maurice Colbeck (as he states *ad nauseam* throughout this book) is the author of *Queer Folk* (Whitethorn Press), all about Yorkshire characters — as well as of *Yorkshire* and *Yorkshire History-makers*. He has recently completed a book about the Yorkshire Dales. After innumerable years as editor of *Yorkshire Life*, he wonders in wilder moments if there might be a world — of sorts — extending for a short distance beyond the Yorkshire boundaries (pre-1974, of course).

THE ARTIST

Albin Trowski was born in Danzig-Gdansk and so can be forgiven for living in what Colbeck calls 'Bigger Manchester'. Having now seen Colbeck's County, Albin plans to apply for political asylum and to that end is receiving language lessons in Broken Yorkshire, these to be followed in due course, by tuition in Mended Yorkshire.

After 30 years residence here, Albin remains an anglophile, but his Scots wife, Laura (also an artist), hopes on bravely that 'some day they'll find a cure'.

ACKNOWLEDGEMENTS

For help in the preparation of this book I am indebted to many people, including Mrs. Kathleen M. Battye, Mr. Derek Bamforth, Mr. Derrick Boothroyd, Mr. Roger Brayshaw, Mr. Harry East, Mr. Wylbert Kemp, Mr. John La Page, Mr. George Taylor (sadly no longer with us), Mrs. A. M. Barritt, for patient and enthusiastic help in checking, typing and retyping, and to various librarians, especially the assiduous Ian Dewhirst.

Chapters 12, 13 and 14, or parts of them, have already appeared, sometimes in different form, in *Yorkshire Life*.

CONTENTS

1 Mind thi own Business **6**

2 Bowdykites, Boggarts and a bit about Baildon **11**

3 Lancastrians and other Queer Folk **17**

4 In the Midst of Life . . . **27**

5 Tyketalk — a Guide for Visitors **34**

6 Can You Insult a Yorkshireman? **48**

7 A Glorious Company **53**

8 The Happy Heart of Cricket **59**

9 Hamlet, or t' Prince o' Lupset **68**

10 Wimmin! Or Sex in Yorkshire **75**

11 Oh, Brother Jucundus! **81**

12 Comical Capital **86**

13 The Infernal Triangle **94**

14 But Don't you *Dare* Laugh at Heckmondwike! **99**

Mind thi own business!

You don't *have* to be a Yorkshireman to have a sense of humour, but I tend to think that if you lack a risible faculty you're at least more likely to be something else.

Fun flourishes in Yorkshire because here are all the necessary conditions. It thrives both in the bracing air of the Dales and in the towns where oppression and poverty once *forced* people to blow away on gales of mirth the neuroses they could not afford . . .

But this is getting too serious. Let me just say that the better-off you are and the farther south you live, the less you are likely to know about humour!

And you need not take my unsupported word for that. In *My Moorland Patients,* a classic of its kind, R. W. S. Bishop says, 'The Yorkshire moorlander possesses a native wit and humour peculiarly his own . . . whereas his Derbyshire brother is as heavy as lead, without a particle of wit or humour in his composition . . . A joke which in Yorkshire would be sure of appreciation is either not understood across the border, or mistaken for an insult.'

Bishop, who had practised in both counties, said he found this humorous faculty, or lack of it, 'nearly as reliable as a map' in establishing one's whereabouts.

But — and now I really take my life in my hands — he also found that even in Yorkshire there were variations and that the moorlanders of the Pennine Range were 'incomparably more witty and humorous than those of the Wolds, or of the Cleveland Hills and the moorlands of North-east Yorkshire'.

Ho'd on a bit! We share the Pennines with Lancashire and it might be inferred that a Pennine *Lancastrian* could just be superior in wit to a native of the East Riding or the North York Moors. And that, as they would readily tell you, 'would nivver do!'

However, now that the Lancastrians have crept in it becomes necessary yet again to put them in their place. To be honest — and I'd never dream of saying this in Bolton — they're not a *bad* lot, but it would be ridiculous ever to say they're simply 'Yorkshiremen who talk a bit funny'.

They're a soft lot really! In saying that I don't impugn their manhood, nor do I cast doubt on their sanity — it's their hearts, not their heads, I'm thinking of — and where better to be soft than there? And along with the kindness there's a moiety of melancholy — it must be something to do with all that rain they need to make the cotton mills work.

They might not *really* be kinder than Yorkshiremen, but my observation, and I've studied 'em for years and years, suggests that they're more likely to wear their soft-heartedness on their collective sleeve than keep it, like the Yorkshireman, in an inside pocket.

Compare the native dialect writers who speak for the two counties. For Yorkshire, John Hartley, say, or Bill o' th' Hoylus End spring to mind — jaunty, irreverent immortals in their own small sphere, but for poverty-stricken dignity and simple heroic humanity how do they compare with Samuel Laycock who, while unemployed, wrote that cotton famine classic *Welcome Bonny Brid* to greet the birth of his third child?

> *Tha'rt welcome, little bonny brid*
> *But shouldn't ha' come just when tha did;*
> *Times are bad.*
> *We're short o' pobbies for our Joe,*
> *But that, of course, tha didn't know,*
> *Did ta, lad?*

It ends . . .

> *But tho' we've childer two or three,*
> *We'll mak' a bit o' room for thee,*
> *Bless thee, lad!*
> *Tha'rt th' prattiest brid we have i' th' nest,*
> *So hutch up closer to mi breast;*
> *I'm thi dad.*

Your Lancastrian is easier moved to tears, perhaps, but any southerner picking up this book is bound to be downright irritated! What, he will doubtless ask, about the merry wit of yer typical cockney sparrer? Well, what about it? The self-congratulatory jollity of the cockney, I make bold to suggest, would have achieved fame nowhere else but in the capital city which produced, fostered and exploited it!

It's *precisely* because he's a Londoner (no 'maybe' about

it) that he gets away with it — and in what an excruciating accent! How dare he mock at the Yorkshireman's honest rounded vowels and say our national dish is only ba'er pudden, mite (he means 'batter', but ba'er goes down be'er wiv the tourists). Furthermore, cockney wit is incurably class-conscious — 'We may be the lower claarses, but we're funny wiv it!'

Dare I say that the Lancastrian is also a bit class-conscious? Certainly he's more deferential to his 'betters' than the Yorkshireman who is quite rightly unaware that he *has* any betters — at least, until they've proved it.

Nobody knew the Yorkshireman better than the late Richard Blakeborough. Times and Yorkshire have changed since his day, but the Yorkshire character remains the same in essentials.

In one of his books he tells the story of an 'off-comed' vicar, new to a North Riding parish, who was quite displeased by the refusal of the congregation to stand when he entered the church for service.

The vicar — rash man — said he would *make* them stand. The next Sunday, as soon as he reached the vestry door, he announced the hymn; the organist started to play and the congregation found themselves on their feet in spite of themselves.

Triumphantly the vicar marched into church. 'And they'll do that every Sunday', he told his churchwarden proudly. The churchwarden was not convinced. 'We deean't tak' kindly to bein' tricked', he warned.

Next Sunday, having given out the hymn, the vicar waited until the music was in full swing before leaving the vestry to enter the church — where he found the congregation singing lustily — but still seated to a man!

Many a parson must have found his first days in a Yorkshire parish trying, to say the least — *truly* trying, for he was the one being tried.

'Why do you never come to church, Metcalfe?' asked the 'superior' but ill-mannered new vicar visiting one of his parishioners.

'Cos Ah'm a Methodist an' Ah go to t' chapel'.

'But they don't teach sound doctrine at the chapel, you know,' said the vicar.

''Appen not,' said Metcalfe,' but they teach yer to tak' yer 'at off when yer go into other folks' 'ouses.'

But there have been parsons in Yorkshire who have been fully equal to their parishioners. One of them, known for his generosity, had descended the stairs after visiting a sick parishioner. Thinking the vicar had left the house, the sufferer called to his wife, 'What's t'owd divil left?'

'T'owd divil's left nowt,' called back the vicar, 'an' he wean't do nawther!'

That last story perhaps illustrates what *is* different about Yorkshire humour — there's an element of aggression there that you don't find everywhere. But there's little malice in our joking — so any leaden-witted Derbyshire chaps who've somehow been holding this book the right way up and wondering if I really meant all

those nasty things can breathe again; lachrymose Lancastrians can dry their tears; choleric cockneys can stop tearing off their pearl buttons and screaming 'Cor strike a light!' Because I'm not saying these things to be unkind — they just happen to be true.

It's usual for authors to express indebtedness to their sources, but here I'm in some difficulty. Where I've quoted original remarks I've acknowledged the author in the text. But most of these stories have no known authorship — they have grown out of the life of Yorkshire itself.

That being the case, you're bound to have heard some of them before, and since chestnuts are inevitable, let's start off with one that's a right conker, but unbeatable as an expression of the 'special relationship' Yorkshire and Lancashire enjoy and their attitude to those less fortunate. It concerns the southerner at a Roses match at Headingley who was applauding a brilliant piece of play when the man on his left enquired, 'Dosta coom fra Lancashire?'

'Who, me? Good gracious no!'

''Appen tha comes from Yorkshire', suggested the man on his right.

'Whatever gave you that idea?'

'Then' (in unison from both right and left) 'mind thi own flamin' business!'

And if you're a Yorkshireman that's my advice to you. So read on — there are sure to be some you *hadn't* heard, and humour is very much a Yorkshireman's business. So mind it! Think on . . .

Bowdykites, Boggarts and a bit about Baildon

What puzzles most Yorkshiremen is the inability of the average *non*-Yorkshireman to understand plain English.

For instance, if I tell you that you are a bowdykite, probably suffering from laikin' fever and for ever bauboskin' about, would you take it as a compliment?

You shouldn't really. Because I'm only telling you that you are a fat, idle good-for-nothing, much given to aimless wandering.

If I were feeling less polite, I might call you a dosselheead or even a daft dunder-heeaded feeal (or fooil, depending on whether I'm in the West or the North Riding).

How should you reply to such a pleasantry?

You could, of course, get all narky and say, 'How dare you compare my mental capacity to that of the knob on top of a corn stack?' (for that's what dossel means). But I wouldn't advise it.

You see, that would fully entitle me to enquire what you were chuntering and threaping about, implying that you were at least a peevish, contradictious taistrell, if not a ragabash, stracklin or fustilugs.

And if your reaction proved that you were really deserving of such a rebuke, we might even come to blows — in which case you might skelp me over the nappercracker, or even fetch me a reight fullock, thus obliging me to give you a proper basting. Or, should that prove inadequate, a twilting, towelling or lacing. (And if you can't work out for yourself what all that means, you deserve raddling, if not bussacking!)

You might say you've no time to listen to such blather, or suggest that my tale is something of an over-long, repetitious paddy-noddy, and that you must be off to your tea. Don't be surprised, then, if I say you are a chaudy guts to be so obsessed with food, and warn you lest your eyes prove bigger than your belly. If I'm right, you might well finish your tea feeling anything but as fit as a lopp (flea, to you) — proper dowly in fact!

But whatever you do, don't stand there ditherin' an' dotherin'. Make up your mind — you mun eether come or go.

Having recovered from the ditherum-dotherums and decided that the whole matter is nobbut a niff-naff and not worth tewing and maddling about, you might stop being so abstracklous and listen to this little tale I am now about to unfold, partly *in the vernacular*. (If you insist on demonstrating your Yorkshire wit, you must now retort — 'Aye, we 'ad one but t' wheel coom off.')

Dialect, alas, is not what it was. It disappeared along with the boggarts, who all spoke the purest and broadest Yorkshire — which gives me an irresistible opportunity to tell you the story of Yorkshire's most famous boggart of all. So pin back your lug'oils an' listen!

Boggart is really a West Riding word, for North Riding folk called them hobmen.

These creatures, who might also have been met with in other parts of England, where they were known as brownies, or in Ireland, where they were called leprechauns, were very useful indeed — but only when they had a mind to be.

What, you might ask, does a boggart or hobman, look like?

It would be easy to give you the quick answer — 'Like a Lancastrian'. But whilst there are undoubted similarities this might prove to be misleading. And at this point I feel I should make it clear that the present writer has no sympathy with that point of view which holds that the entire population of Lancashire is composed of boggarts!

This, emphatically, is not the case. I have, in fact, known several Lancastrians who could prove their human origin by their descent from authenticated Yorkshire stock. (It's just that boggarts attract less notice in Lancashire and mingle more easily with the native population.)

Well then, what *are* they like? But why should you take the word of a mere commoner like me! Listen instead to what a king — James VI no less — had to say about them. He called them brownies — but make sure you do not confuse them with those Brownies who are the tadpoles of Girl Guides, much given, I believe, to dib-dibbing, dob-dobbing, campfire songs, forcing old ladies to cross the road, and other good works.

'A brownie', said His Gracious Majesty, 'is a rough man, haunts without doing any evil, doing necessary turns up and down the house.' Some were so blinded as to believe that a house was all the sonsier (by which the poor, misguided Scotian meant tidier) when such spirits resided there.

All of which suggests to me that King Jim had never met a real Yorkshire boggart, or he would have been unable to recite such complacent rubbish for shaking in his Scottish shoes.

Your genuine boggart, according to the best authorities, is half a man (which would, of course, make him approximately a quarter of a Yorkshireman).

As recently as 1820 a farming family, called Oughtred, who lived near Hob Hill, Upleatham, were fortunate enough — at least at first — to have a hobman living nearby who was apparently 'niver stalled o' wark'. In other words, he was allus agate on some job or another — tending cattle, threshing corn, digging ditches, topping and tailing turnips. Thee name it — he could do it. Nothing was too hard for him and everything was fine — at first... But boggarts or hobmen (call 'em whatever tha's a mind to) are allus varry ready to tak' t' hig (or as foreigners might say, take offence). And if there's one certain way to upset them, it is to offer them clothing or shoes. Don't ask me why, but if there's one thing that

invariably puts a boggart's back up it's the suggestion that he should put summat on it!

Just *what* farmer Oughtred did has never been known for certain, but it's believed that he may have hung his coat on the winnowing machine and forgotten to take it away with him when he returned to the house...

He could have done nothing more disastrous! Because when the hobman found the coat late that night he felt certain it was intended for him.

From that moment on the hobman morally went into reverse! Instead of baking bread, he burnt it. He would toss people out of bed, turn the milk sour, let the animals loose or scatter dung on the parlour floor. Life soon became unbearable and the family decided to flit.

A new farm was bought as speedily as possible and all preparations made. By the time everything was packed up and the family settled down for their last night at the old place, they were just about worn out. At least the hobman could no longer toss them out of bed, because their beds were all rolled up on the wagon outside.

And so they lay, on mattresses on the floor, waiting for the nightly torment to begin.

But for some reason it never did, and the family found the silence so unaccustomed that they wondered if they wouldn't sleep better if the hobman *did* get up to some of his old tricks again!

By morning, however, they were in rather a forgiving mood, mellowed by sentimental regret at leaving t'owd place, the scene of so much family happiness.

At last all was ready and the family climbed aboard the wagon.

'Ee, lass,' said the farmer, as he cracked his whip, 'Ah ommost wish we wor stoppin' ere!'

'Ah know just 'ow tha feels', said his wife, 'but just think 'ow grand it'll be to get away from yond hobman.'

Just then, a neighbour who was rather out of touch with events saw the family on the wagon and called: 'Ah *say*, ye're not flittin *sewerly!*'

Instantly the lid of a milk can at the goodwife's side was lifted from within, and a small brown head appeared.

'Aye, we're flittin', said the hobman.

'Tha'd better turn t' wagon round, lad', said the farmer's wife to her good man. 'We mud as weel stop wheer we are.'

They tell similar boggart tales in Lancashire, but they may well be copies of Yorkshire stories and you'd be well advised not to give them too much credence. (Quite frankly, some of them are just a bit unbelievable.)

Boggarts and the like were rather choosy about their stamping grounds. They seem to have had a soft spot, for instance, for Baildon. And not only boggarts — there was also the Guytrash, a ghostly hound whose appearance presaged evil, and his close relation, the Padifooit, who was particularly fond of haunting Baildon's Westgate area. Nor must we forget Bloodiboans, who had his territory in Tentercroft, while Chatterchains lived in the rocks under Baildon Bank.

I look for them every time I visit Baildon, but the nearest I've been to meeting one was seeing *Dracular was hear* chalked on a gravestone.

But Baildon's boggarts must have been hard put to it to compete with some of the human characters I heard about once from Baildon's own historian, John La Page . . .

Characters like Black Joe, who won a 'fahlest face' contest without even trying; like Bill Boocock, who strapped on a pair of goosewings and tried to fly. He fell, of course, because, as his friends pointed out, 'Tha niver flapped'; like Jack Holmes, who promised a new hat to anyone who would bathe every Sunday morning up to Christmas in Spink Well. And like Sam Bentley, who won the hat, even though he had to break the ice on Christmas morning.

Baildoners apparently used to pride themselves on being lazy. They once asked the vicar to arrange for them to have two Sundays a week. One day, one of the gentry, passing through Baildon on horseback, said he would give a shilling to the idlest of three men he met playing marbles. All three claimed the honour; the visiting toff made his choice and held out the coin.

'Nay', said the winner, 'tha mun come and put it in mi pocket.'

Lancastrians and other Queer Folk

No Yorkshireman has been on his blessed native soil long before he learns to his astonishment that there are other people, less fortunate than himself, who were actually *born in other counties!*

Indeed, it comes as quite a shock to learn that there *are* other counties, because it's quite obvious, that Yorkshire on its own could supply all essentials for civilized living, such as Test teams and black puddings (ignore claims by envious Lancastrians that they have invented or discovered this delicacy, which as every Yorkshire child knows comes from the world-famous black pudding mines near Pudsey).

Yorkshire has also coal, iron, potash and Pontefract cakes. Not to mention best bitter and the sort of high-quality boiled ham that no self-respecting Yorkshireman would dream of being buried without. We have dales and mountains, a hundred miles of coastline and major ports like Hull (which every Yorkshireman will tell you is still in the East Riding and not in some imaginary county called Humberside).

However, the workings of Providence (though unquestionably a Yorkshireman) were ever inscrutable and we have to face the fact that these strange denizens of other counties do exist.

Are they truly human?

Do they have a purpose?

Are they descended from the crew of a forgotten spaceship lost on earth when the solar system was young?

Thus we question ourselves — if we are daft enough. Are they heck, we answer in almost every case. Actually, there is very little that we really *know* about them, except that they are A Queer Lot.

First in order of Queerness come *Foreigners,* whose limited knowledge of English makes them think that a Barnsley chop is concerned with a Yorkshire form of karate; that Goole is a kind of morbid Yorkshire ghost and Ilkley Moor, Henry's younger brother. They can hardly be blamed for such ignorance, having come from foreign places ovver t'watter. But there is far less excuse for native-born Englishmen, even if they are of the variety known as *Southerners*.

The true Yorkshireman needs little warning to steer clear of this strange variety, given to bowler-hat-wearing, umbrella-carrying, and torturing the English language in their speech.

Now for Lancastrians, who can only be judged in relation to Yorkshireman to whom they are a kind of 'spoiled lot', the clumsy product of a 'prentice hand. Yorkshireman (as they themselves can tell you) are God's *élite,* the cream not just of England but of the world — generous, industrious, highly intelligent . . . And anyone who says they're not is probably a Lancastrian.

Not that Yorkshiremen look down on Lancastrians. Well, they do, of course, but from a less dizzy eminence perhaps, and in a kindlier way than they look down on the rest of mankind. Indeed, the Yorkshireman sees the fellows who live across the Pennines as generally superior to the rest of *Non-*Yorkshire — as Yorkshiremen *manqué* or (in plain terms understandable even in Bolton) as Yorkshiremen that didn't quite come off.

A dream of the future?
No, just a Yorkshireman's nightmare!

Nor, let me tell you, are the Lankies unaware of it! Otherwise they would not have the temerity — impudence might be a better word — to boast about their prowess at cricket, a game in which their rules entitle them to 'cheat fair' by fielding a team that might include Indians, West Indians or renegade Yorkshiremen; whereas even a Lancastrian knows that to play cricket for Yorkshire you have to be born there.

So much for Lesser Breeds without the Law. Yet in a world already peopled with oddities in such abundance and variety it will probably come as no small surprise to you to learn that there are Queer Folk even in the ranks of Yorkshire folk. And when Yorkshire folk are queer, they're better at it than most.

Some of these have already been discussed in an admirable volume called *Queer Folk,* the identity of whose author the present writer must conceal for reasons of modesty. Suffice it to say that the incredible smallness of its price has caused more than one fatality from shock among Yorkshire customers, who sometimes over-react to a bargain.

For those equal to the intellectual challenge involved, let me say that *Queer Folk* concerns itself with such as Bill Sharp, of Keighley, who went to bed for 50 years when his girl failed to turn up for their wedding; Jonathan Martin, who set fire to York Minster for religious reasons: Jemmy Hirst, of Rawcliffe, who taught a duck to swim backwards and a rooster to dance to his mouth organ accompaniment; he also rode a bull to hounds and wore a hat nine feet in circumference. (But if I tell you any more about Jemmy it might spoil your enjoyment of *Queer Folk*).

Even that excellent and comprehensive volume, however, could not contain *all* Yorkshire's Queer Folk, who, as I say, excel in number and the standard of their eccentricity the Queer Folk of any other county.

I have, in fact, actually defended this claim in enemy territory! It was an interviewer for Radio Manchester who issued the challenge and when, doubtless to his astonishment, I accepted it, he said with a curl of his Lancastrian lip that he had expected me, as a Yorkshireman, to be green in colour and equipped with antennae.

With a flash of the devastating and original wit for which we are so famous I retorted that I had expected the very same of him! He staggered, picked himself up from the studio floor, readjusted the earphones which I had thought part of his head, and continued as best he could. His benighted listeners phoned in of course with their own somewhat pathetic stories which bore no comparison with those of our idiosyncratic giants (featured in the modest author's book mentioned above).

That expedition across the Pennines, reminiscent, perhaps, of the great missionary journeys of St. Paul, was not without its benefits to the less enlightened of our race — you can now buy copies of *Queer Folk* at certain Manchester hot-dog stands, where the flame of culture flickers as the sausages sizzle and, of course, from all good book shops (and is there any other kind?) in Yorkshire.

One thing for which Yorkshiremen are frequently and unjustly condemned by those less venturesome or less fortunate is their remarkable capacity to turn to profit any natural peculiarities of appearance or manner. Take, for instance, the wonderful ability to impersonate that hon. Yorkshireman Mike Yarwood, demonstrated both by the Poet Laureate of Upandunder, Professor Eddie Waring, and that genius in a Gannex, our former Prime Minister, H. Wilson (Kt.).

But there have been others in humbler spheres who have used their personal oddities to turn an honest bob or penny — in one case almost literally. I refer to Old Boots, described as follows in the *Wonderful Magazine* of March 1st, 1793:

This extraordinary man lived long at an inn (The Unicorn) at Ripon in Yorkshire. By nature and habit he acquired the power of holding a piece of money between his nose and chin. His chief employment was waiting on the customers and from the circumstance of his cleaning their shoes and boots he went by the name of Old Boots.

You don't meet characters like that any more, except in Lancashire, perhaps, where the natural rapacity of the natives incites them to seize and hold on to coin of the realm by whatever means presents itself, and then try to ease their consciences by accusing Yorkshiremen of being mean.

Behold, a Giant — and Jack Lob

William Bradley knew how to make the best of what nature had bestowed. If you want to know what that was take a look inside the Londesborough Arms at Market Weighton, where you will see a picture of William with two 'ordinary' men who reach to somewhere near his bottom waistcoat button.

William, you see, was the Market Weighton 'giant', who was reduced (if that's the word) to travelling the country with a giant pig in order to earn his living.

William was a 'big lad' from the start. He weighed fully a stone at his birth in 1787 to John and Ann Bradley who had 11 children in all but probably came to the conclusion that they would have had enough with William on his own.

The lad grew and grew. At the age of 11 he weighed as many stones. After leaving school he worked for some years as a farm labourer, but when he was 21 he joined a travelling showman and in company with his porcine parallel, 'The Yorkshire Pig', toured the country.

He weighed 27 stones now and stood 7 ft. 9 ins. in his 15 inch-long shoes. He was enough of a Yorkshireman to realize that he could perhaps make more money by managing his own affairs. Here is the handbill he had printed to announce his visit to Hull Fair in 1815:

> To be seen during the Fair, at the house, No. 7 Queen Street, Mr. Bradley, the most wonderful and surprising Yorkshire Giant, 7 feet 9 inches high, weighs 27 stones, who has had the honour of being introduced to Their Majesties and Royal Family at Windsor, where he was most

graciously received. A more surprising instance of gigantic stature has never been beheld or exhibited in any other Kingdom, being proportionate in all respects, the sight of him never fails to give universal gratification and will fill the beholders' eyes with wonder and astonishment. He is allowed by the greatest judges to Surpass all men ever yet seen. Admittance one shilling.

Considering what the value of one shilling must have been in 1815, William probably did very nicely out of it, financially at least. Let us hope so, because he had little luck in other directions. Like many another big man he had poor health and so had to give up the travelling life and return to Market Weighton.

But now a problem arose: where was the 'giant' to live? He had to bend almost double to enter the door of any house. The home he had specially built, with high doors and ceilings, must have been almost as much a marvel in Market Weighton as William himself had been. And still was, though now a lame, pathetic figure, supporting his huge frame with the aid of a seven-foot crutch and a walking stick four feet long.

He did not enjoy his outsize house for long. He died in 1820 aged about 33, and his coffin, measuring nine feet by three, was interred in Market Weighton churchyard in the early hours, to foil the body-snatchers of the day: they could have asked a high price from surgeons for such a novelty among corpses! As a further safeguard the poor giant was disinterred and reburied within the church itself.

Poor William was among the 'queer folk' through no fault of his own, you might say, and perhaps he was a subject more fitting for tears than for laughter. There were others in Yorkshire about that time who probably caused more vexation than mirth in their lifetime, though in retrospect people have found it easy enough to laugh at them.

Jack Lob was one of those — an apparently gormless character whose daftness never got in the way of his own advantage.

His real name was John Robinson and he lived in the Bingley area. Like that of many another oddity, his behaviour became the subject of public mirth only after tragedy had visited his life.

Jack had fetched some treacle to sweeten his father's porridge when the old man was ill. As he watched him eating it, Jack beseeched him not to 'dee, owd lad'. But, sad to say, that's just what the owd lad did. And of course, Poor Jack Lob felt sure it was the treacle that had killed him! The sense of guilt must have turned his brain.

He became a wandering beggar and the neighbourhood pest. Yet angry as his antics made them, the good folk of Bingley could hardly help laughing. Or at least, some of them! Those most closely concerned were often anything but amused.

For a time Jack yielded to public pressure and got himself a steady job in a coal mine, where one of his duties was to lower other men into the pit.

One day a miner in a hurry got rather impatient.

"Urry up an' let mi dahn, yer daft gawbie! Ah 'aven't got all day', he said — or words to that effect.

So without a word, Jack let go of the rope — and the miner dropped so fast into the pit that he broke both legs.

Afterwards Jack just couldn't understand what all the fuss was about. "E wanted to go down wi' a wallop, so Ah let 'im, full speed, owd lad, full speed,' he explained.

Perhaps poor Jack was less guilty than some of his tormentors. He was always filthy, so one day some warehousemen forcibly gave him a bath in a mill dam and hung him from the top warehouse window to dry.

On another occasion, after stripping naked — for a fee — he allowed himself to be blackened all over . . . and literally frightened a woman to death when he peered through the window of the house where she had just given birth. Not surprisingly, she thought he was the devil.

I'd hazard a guess that perhaps the great difficulty in dealing with Jack was to gauge just how daft he was! Take the day when he helped the miner down the pit. Or the time he killed the snake.

Jack *said* it was a snake. Anybody else would have called it a feather boa of the type popular in those days. Jack saw it lying on the ground and when the wind rustled its feathers, was convinced it was a dangerous serpent.

'Ah'll teych thi to be a snake', Jack warned it severely and proceeded to hurl stones at it. But as long as the wind rustled its feathers Jack was sure it was alive.

'Dee, snake, dee!' he shouted and stamped upon it till it was 'killed'.

When a woman asked Jack if he'd seen anything of her boa he was all ignorance — and innocence.

'Nay, Ah've seen nowt o't'sooart, owd lass', he said. 'Ah did see a big snake — but dooan't worry, Ah killed it wi' a stooan'.

Was Jack 'as daft as he looked'? Not all the time — and there were some who found that out to their cost. Once, offered a penny by a farmer's wife to clean out a farmyard, he demanded payment in advance then walked away with her penny ignoring the parsimonious woman's angry shouts.

Jack had his regular benefactors, but he seems to have treated them no better than he did his exploiters.

'Ah've no change today, Jack, owd lad', said one of them one day, who could usually be relied upon for twopence, 'come back in a bit'. But when Jack returned, the answer was still the same. Jack looked downcast at this. 'Well, 'ere's a tanner', said his friend, 'take your money out an' bring me t'change'.

Jack eventually returned and handed over a penny, explaining to his surprised benefactor: 'Tha owes me tuppence for t'first time, tuppence for this time an' a penny for gettin' it changed'.

Accused in court one day of some offence, all he would say, when questioned, was 'I like plum pudding, beef an' cake'. The court decided he was mad and let him go.

In the Midst of Life . . .

Traditionally the Yorkshireman's sense of occasion comes into its own most of all at funerals. He feels he should celebrate the fact that he, at least, is still here. And time was when no Yorkshireman (or woman) was properly 'sided' without a veritable funeral banquet in which home-fed ham loomed large (though there may have been those who considered black pudding more appropriate).

And funeral protocol was as important as the furnishing of the table. It called for careful discrimination, for instance, to decide who sat with whom in the funeral conveyances.

One mourner at a Dales funeral was obviously prepared to co-operate in every way he could, just to make sure things went with a proper swing!

'An' who', he asked the undertaker, 'does ta want *me* to ride wi'?'

Solemnly that functionary consulted his list. 'Would you', he requested softly, 'please ride with Mrs. Metcalfe?'

The mourner's face fell.

'Ah shan't enjoy miself a *bit* if I 'ave to travel wi' *'er'*, he said. For Mrs. Metcalfe was his mother-in-law.

Bidden to attend the funeral of his friend's third wife, a Yorkshireman declined as graciously as the circumstances seemed to require. As he explained to his own wife: it seemed a bit greedy to keep accepting the hospitality of others when he couldn't return the compliment.

If all the stories you hear are true, Yorkshire must be full of widows who had their husbands cremated and the ashes put in an egg-timer. "E niver worked in his life,' they are apt to say, 'so Ah'll see to it 'e makes up for it now.'

Unfortunately, the cost of funerals has risen to such an extent that as an old woman in Heckmondwike pointed out, 'Folk can't even afford to dee these days!'

But is *living* any cheaper? The Leyburn farmer who had learned with horror the cost of his friend's operation, 'done private', was not so sure.

'Ah'd *niver* 'ave paid all that', he exploded. 'Ah'd a *deed* fust!'

While all due deference must be paid to the dead and the 'deein'', the living, too, are entitled to some small consideration, even in Yorkshire.

''Ow does tha feel today, Joe?' asked Sam of his corpulent friend.

'Nay, Ah'm noan so grand,' said Joe. 'If Ah dooan't mend varry quick, Ah s'll not be 'ere much longer.'

Sam looked at him in alarm 'Ee, tha mun 'ang on, owd lad! Don't give up without a struggle. Tha sees, this 'ouse o'thine is at least five mile fra' t'church and they're sartain to ask me to be one o't'bearers. Tha mun see if tha can't pine away a bit, like, afore tha goes!'

Whether Joe did the decent thing by slimming down to a more convenient weight, we do not know, but let's hope he presented a respectable corpse (unlike the man whose widow refused to pay over the odds to have him shaved ready for his funeral. After all, she opined, he wasn't going anywhere special).

But whatever you do, don't be misled into thinking that Yorkshire folk take death more lightly than others and are less desolated by the loss of a partner. As one bereaved moorland farmer, surprised by his own grief, put it, he'd sooner 'ave shot t'owd dog. (Perhaps he was the husband who asked his wife where she'd like to be buried and got the answer he deserved: 'On top o' thee!')

But what of the afterlife? How does the contemplation of the heavenly mansions strike one who has spent his life among the lovely vistas of the Dales? When an earnest lady tried to impart some notion of the joys of Paradise, the dying Dalesman felt he must save her any unnecessary exertion.

''Appen yer don't know this', he whispered confidentially, 'but Ah once went to t'pantomime at Leeds, so I 'ave gotten some idea what it'll be like.'

Yorkshiremen are kindly at heart, but they sometimes deserve the reputation they have earned for being unforgiving. Even so, death can change most things. Jim and Bill had lived as next-door neighbours beside a Yorkshire village green for 40 years but during most of that time never a word or a look had they exchanged, though both had probably forgotten what their original quarrel was about.

Then came the time Jim learned his days were numbered. The two men's friends couldn't bear to see the quarrel still unhealed and after much hard talking persuaded Jim to invite his neighbour in.

'They say Ah'm deein', an' if they're reight tha can consider our difference is settled,' said the old man as he lay stolidly in bed. Many times Bill had secretly longed to heal the breach but dared not say so. A glad smile lit up his features: eagerly he held out his hand . . .

Too eagerly, perhaps, for Jim! With a startled look he withdrew his own hands beneath the counterpane. *'That's* if Ah dee, tha understands,' he said coolly. 'Don't expect any alteration if Ah get better!'

A somewhat rascally gamekeeper, having had his leg amputated after an accident, had it laid in a special oak box and tried in vain to persuade one parson after another to read the funeral service over it. Finally, when the time came, it was buried beside him.

'Did he really try an' get his leg buried separate?' asked one of the mourners.

''E did an' all', was the answer. ''E said 'e didn't intend to wakken up i' Heaven short of a leg. But if tha asses me it wor a waste o' time, cos that bugger's sartin to ave gooan straight to 'ell if onnybody ivver did.'

While on the subject of death, Yorkshire is famous for two somewhat funereal compositions — one serious, the chilling Lyke Wake Dirge which describes the purgatorial passage of the soul after death over the mythical Whinny Moor, the other lugubriously comical — *On Ilkla 'Moor Baht 'At*. Today the former is commemorated by the 40-mile Lyke Wake Walk undertaken by hundreds every year over wild moorland between Osmotherley and Ravenscar on the coast. But 200 and more years ago it was chanted over corpses in North Yorkshire in anticipation of the journey the soul was undertaking:

> *This yah neet, this yah neet,*
>   *Ivvery neet an' all,*
> *Fire an' sleet an' candle leet,*
>   *An' Christ tak' up thi soul*
>
> *When thoo fra hither gans away,*
>   *Ivvery neet an' all,*
> *Ti Whinny Moor thoo cumst at last,*
>   *An' Christ tak' up thi soul*
>
> *If ivver thou gavest hosen or shoon,*
>   *Ivvery neet an' awl,*
> *Clap tha doon an' put 'em on,*
>   *An' Christ tak' up thi soul*

Then we shall all

> *But if hosen an' shoon thoo niver ga' neean,*
> *Ivvery neet an' all*
> *T'whinnies [thorns] 'll prick thi sair to t'beean*
> *An' Christ tak' up thi soul*

And so it goes on: the soul is tested at point after point and if found wanting stands in danger of the direst consequences:

> *If siller or gowd thoo niver gave neean ...*
> *Thou'll doon, doon tummle towards hell's fleeams.*

No need for a translation, I think: there is something in the haunting rhythm that seems to transcend the strangeness of the dialect.

Hardly a subject for Yorkshire laughter, I agree. But perhaps it makes a useful contrast to the most famous Yorkshire ditty of all, sung wherever exiles from the Broad Acres meet; the song that has made one part of Yorkshire famous the world over — *Ilkla' Moor Baht 'At*.

It has been described as a hymn to pessimism, a declaration in song about the pointlessness of it all! And that, if I may say so, is a load of rubbish — it's just another example of the Yorkshireman's refusal to take death and the last things too seriously.

There are several accounts of its origin and one is no doubt as good as another.

One says that a 19th-century chapel choir from Milnsbridge, or somewhere, had chosen to take a chara' trip to Ilkley. When they returned from a venturesome walk on the moor, the first tenor was unaccountably

missing just when the choirmaster decided to favour Ilkley with the choicest items from their repertoire.

What was more to the point, the choirmaster's daughter, Mary Jane, was missing, too — no laughing matter in Father's eyes!

When the couple finally reappeared, the first tenor's hair was ruffled, his face was flushed and — most suspicious circumstance of all — his billy cock was missing . . . Doubtless, as the anthem tells, he'd been 'a-courtin' Mary Jane'!

And so, on their way home, the choir, with lungs invigorated by moorland air, improvised the legend to an already familiar hymn tune, *Cranbrook* (which is still sung in the North to the Christmas hymn *While Shepherds Watched Their Flocks by Night*).

It would be nice to know whether Mary Jane and her father and the first tenor joined in the singing, and whether they lived happily ever after, but alas we never shall. All we have is the song, uniquely 'Yorkshire', whether you like it or not.

For the benefit of foreigners and any Yorkists who might (perish the thought) be equally ignorant, I give the lyric in a summarised form together with a translation into what is called standard English:

Wheer 'as tha been sin' Ah saw thee
On Ilkla' Moor baht 'at?
(Where have you been since I saw you on Ilkley Moor with your head all unprotected against the elements?)
Wheer, etc. (repeated)
On Ilkla' Moor, etc. (repeated ... three times!)

Tha're bahn to catch thi deeath o' cowd
(I fear you will suffer from your rashness and may even perish from the effects of exposure)
On Ilkla' moor, etc (repeated ... three *more* times!)

Then t' wurrms 'll coom an' eyt thi oop, etc.
(After your demise, your mortal remains will be consumed by invertebrates of the worm family, which in turn will be devoured by ducks, the ducks being consumed in due course by ourselves.)

Then we shall all 'ave etten thee, etc
(Then we shall all 'ave etten thee, etc.)

It's said that in 1929 Philip Snowden retaliated with this cannibalistic dirge, Yorkshire's far-from-secret weapon, against a musical assault by Welsh songsters while he was a guest of Lloyd George at Churt. (In spite of that, he lived to become Viscount Snowden.)

Our so-called anthem has been translated into Danish *(Paa himmel-bjerget uden hat)* and Russian. Cheshire and Lancashire have tried to pinch it, inserting 'Mottram Edge' or 'Oldham Edge' in place of Ilkla' Moor.

It's also been claimed to be a corruption of a French or German drinking song — but that was mostly by Yorkshiremen, understandably eager to give it away ...

Tyketalk — a guide for visitors

Try enquiring the way to the Wharfedale village of Appletreewick and you, as a mere foreigner, might well be asked by a superior-mannered local, 'Ah suppose tha means Aptrick?' If, heeding my warning, you ask initially for 'Aptrick' you will undoubtedly be asked if you are not really seeking Appletreewick.

All of which suggests that, faced with the Yorkshireman's natural-born awk'ardness (amounting in its highest flights to genius), the foreigner might have difficulty in establishing his whereabouts.

And this of course is quite true. The best you can hope to do is outdo the fellow at his own game — possibly by asking the way to The-Hamlet-Bearing-The-Name-of-a-Certain-Fructuous-Tree. But I don't advise it. Yorkshiremen have a knack of dealing most effectively with smart-alecs like you!

For example, a Londoner, who had lost his way, asked a Yorkshire lad the way to Pickering, only to be told, 'Nay, *Ah* doan't know'. Neither did the lad know how far it was, or anything else that the visitor might have found in the least helpful.

'What, the hell,' demanded the visitor in some exasperation, *'do you know?'*

The countryman thought about it for a moment. 'Ah know Ah'm not lost', he said at last.

And if *you* are not to be lost in Yorkshire you should find out certain things — for instance, where to go and what the blazes they're talking about when you get there.

Where, you might ask, do I find the true heart of Yorkshire? Where is the Yorkshire tongue spoken in unsullied purity? Where do Yorkshire characteristics flourish most strongly? And where is Yorkshire scenery to be enjoyed at its most awe-inspiring?

And, unhesitatingly, I give you the answer in one word — Batley. Yes, you heard me. But fearlessly I repeat it (in capitals this time) — BATLEY.

Let cowards flinch and traitors sneer; let Dewsbury men deny the truth of my assertion, so long as they don't persuade you that any other place has such a claim to be the heart of Yorkshire. That heart *is* Batley. You can take my word for it. How do I know? That's easy — I was born there. And to any Yorkshireman, the place of his birth is indisputably the heart of Yorkshire.

Visiting film-makers, engaged on epics which might now be called *Carry on up the Calder,* have compared some of Batley's finest vistas with probable aspects of hell; they have speculated on the suitability of Batley Cemetery as a backcloth for Dracula films. But who are they to judge? (Come to think of it, Batley is very probably not just the heart of Yorkshire, but of the world . . . if not the universe!)

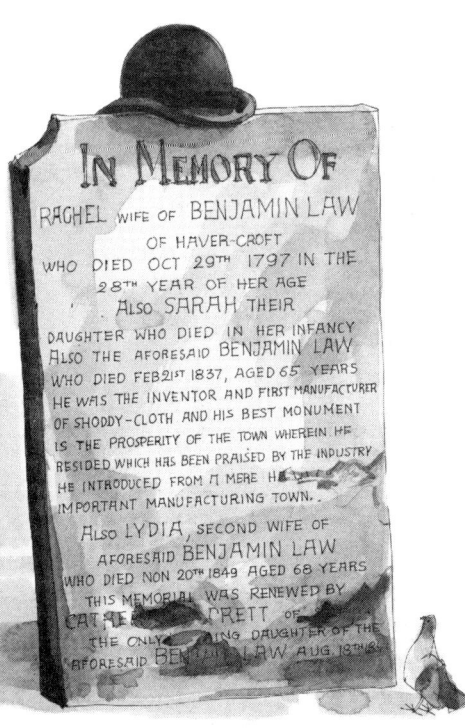

Derrick Boothroyd, whose novel they were filming, was born in Leeds but soon emigrated to Batley, so he knows. Not for nothing is his latest book called *Nowt So Queer As Folk*. And what memories of Batley it recalls!

Any one of its inimitable characters could have told you that they made Batley and Batley made them. The two-way process has continued since the day Benjamin Law (whose tombstone may still be read in the churchyard of the 15th century All Saints Church) invented shoddy. Oh yes, Batley is an ancient place — the Romans knew it, though there is much less evidence of their presence in the place than there is of Benjamin Law's.

Those mills which still remain from Batley's great days speak of what Ben got up to, but the worn lettering of his tombstone tells the story rather more explicitly.

He was, it says, *the inventor and first manufacturer of shoddy cloth . . . His best monument is the prosperity of the town . . . which has been raised from a mere hamlet to an important manufacturing town.*

Dewsbury has no Benjamin Law and don't let them tell you they have.

But *how* did Ben transform the mere hamlet into the important town? Simple: he invented shoddy cloth and began making it in 1813.

Only a Batley man could have invented shoddy manufacture. Ben did it (in the simplest terms) by grinding down woollen rags and mixing the resultant tangle with virgin wool. Thus, for the first time in history, he made woollen clothing cheap enough for the working man to afford.

But we are less interested in social revolution just now than in the characters who followed in Ben's woolly wake.

I first learnt about them in my childhood: their legends were part of every Batley lad's heritage then, though I doubt if they will much longer survive the mills they built. We soon learned that the proper name for Zion Methodist Church was the Shoddy Temple, because that was where the woollen manufacturers worshipped God in between dancing attendance on Mammon.

And who can blame the exploited mill-workers for getting their own back on their often grasping bosses in the only way open to them — by laughing at them! And many of them were certainly laughable enough.

With some outstanding exceptions they were not invariably men of taste and culture. After all, they had not themselves enjoyed the education they were now rich enough to inflict on their sons. But having come up in the world they were determined to accept nothing less than the best.

It *may not* have been a Batley mill-owner who called his palatial residence The Cloisters, because it was cloise ter t' mill, cloise ter t' pub an' cloise ter t' station, but there can be little doubt the tale originated in the town.

Could it have been the same man who, having been told by the architect of his proposed mansion that every house had 'an aspect', told the architect to give him three?

The mill men used their money to carve their way to acceptance and respectability, and you denied them membership of your golf club at your peril. So rejected, one of them bought the site of the club and demanded election under threat of evicting the club. They elected him, but he never played there, perhaps because any further victory — less than a hole-in-one — would have been rather an anti-climax.

Hell, Hull and . . . Huddersfield?

You are no doubt familiar with the Thieves' Litany (which is all that some foreigners know about Yorkshire). It goes
— *From Hell, Hull and Halifax, good Lord deliver us.*

Hull may have been considered a place to avoid because of the danger of transportation from there; but there can be no argument about the reason for including Halifax in the litany.

Time was when they lopped off your head here on an early model of the Guillotine they called the gibbet just for stealing cloth worth more than 13½d. And why not, indeed? We're far too soft nowadays, probably because so many Lancastrian Liberals have got into Parliament.

Due no doubt to their being such big soft Lancastrian nellies, this salutary practice has now almost died out, but in quite recent years the original gibbet blade was discovered, so we are quite likely to reintroduce the practice at any time. But do not, dear Lancastrian reader, alarm yourself. Such as you will be quite safe (on the grounds of diminished responsibility) and the only people in real danger will be difficult southerners and people from Huddersfield.

Incidentally, there are those who say that the Thieves' Litany actually originated in Huddersfield, where they changed it, chucking in Hull and Hell (*not* a part of Yorkshire, whatever they say in Bolton) just to divert suspicion from themselves.

Huddersfield, you see, is Halifax's nearest comparable neighbour and in Yorkshire the traditional way to regard the denizens of neighbouring towns is as raving idiots.

Thus Batley has always poured scorn upon Dewsbury, a practice which reaches its climax once a year when the neighbouring towns' young men attempt to dismember each other publicly under a thin pretence of playing Rugby League, a game whose patron saint, one E. Waring, comes from the latter soot-stained town. Thus Guiseley folk call Yeadon Dozytown — or did; Marsden is 'wheer they black-leead t' tram lines' — but only, I repeat, to its neighbours.

In Batley the birds 'fly back'ards to keep the muck out of their eyes'. Or so they say in Morley. It may strike you as a coincidence that the birds in Farsley do precisely the same thing if we are to believe the folk of Pudsey, as indeed, they might well do also in Bradford. The skies of industrial Yorkshire, in fact, must have been full at one time of birds flying backwards.

'Why', you might ask, 'have I never observed this curious phenomenon?' And the answer, which is surely quite obvious, can only be that your own eyes must have been filled with soot at the time.

Nowadays, in our comparatively smokeless Yorkshire skies, there is no need for the birds to fly backwards, which seems a pity because in today's clearer skies it would be so much easier to see them performing this interesting aerial feat.

A Pudsey man, by the way, once denied with some vehemence my suggestion that it was in his own home town that our feathered friends advanced in reverse.

'*Nay,*' he said, 'that wor *Farsley,* an' they flew back'ards cos they didn't care where they were *goin'* — they wanted to know where the 'ell they'd been'.

Whatever the reason they did it, the thought conjures up a spectacle which would have delighted Jemmy Hirst of Rawcliffe, one of our lovable Yorkshire eccentrics, (incidentally, every Yorkshireman is *that* — if you doubt it, just ask him). Jemmy (as fortunate readers of a book called *Queer Folk* are already aware) not only taught a duck to swim backwards but trained a rooster to dance to the tunes of his mouth-organ. Or have I said that?

Pudsey!

One place in Yorkshire inspires a unique respect — Pudsey, which besides being — well — a bit on the quaint side in appearance (and none the worse for that) is a birthplace second-to-none of Yorkshire cricketers.

Any place that had produced John Tunnicliffe, Herbert Sutcliffe, Major Booth, Sir Len Hutton and Ray Illingworth would be certain of veneration in Yorkshire, but somehow Pudsey has been endowed with a dual character — perhaps just to make sure its fame as a cricket nursery doesn't go to its head.

Pudsey, the rest of Yorkshire seems to have decided long ago, is *funny* — though Pudsey itself can't quite see the joke . . . Nor could Wilfred Pickles, who, when he visited Pudsey, declared that he'd looked around the place for something funny but had found nowt. Wilfred, of course, came from Halifax . . . but whether or not you think *that* has any bearing on the matter probably depends on whether or not you come from Huddersfield.

This amusement at Pudsey's expense is nothing new. A hundred years ago we find a local historian observing that the very name of the town 'furnished amusement for many a long year'.

Does this worry Pudsey folk? Not a bit! Their motto is 'Be just and fear not' and indeed why should they fear some of the jokes aimed at them, when the jokers, if judged by some of their own witticisms, were manifestly dafter than their victims.

One exception was the dialect versifier John Hartley, who described the experiences of a certain Parson Drew, who came — yes! — from Pudsey.

Having finally quitted the town, he went to the place where all good parsons might be expected to go, only to find that St. Peter flatly denied the existence of any such place as Pudsey. As far as I can recall, this is what happened next . . .

Being a resourceful sort of parson, the heaven-bound Revd. Mr. Drew had provided himself, somewhat surprisingly, with a map of Yorkshire, by means of which he was able to convince the saint that Pudsey really did exist.

Picture the scene if you will . . . The guardian of the

heavenly gates, obviously more of a wag than he has been given credit for, cups his venerable ear with his saintly hand and asks Parson Drew to state his place of origin.

'Pudsey . . . Pudsey? Can't say t' name means owt to me. Minds tha, there *is* a place in that neighbourhood wheer t' angels keep complainin' o' gettin' soot in their ees when they fly ovver. Could that be it?'

And Parson Drew, if I know him, replied, *'That* 'ud be Farsley. Them angels didn't care wheer they were goin' — they wanted to know wheer the . . . Heckmondwike they'd been'.

In the end St. Peter had no choice but to admit the parson, but he did so grudgingly, warning that

Tha'll find inside noa friends o' thine.
Tha's first 'at's come thro' Pudsey.

But that — as they will tell you in Farsley — is enough about Pudsey.

Pie and chips

They might not be daft in Denby Dale, but they can surely be described as a bit pie-eyed.

Every so often pie fever hits this village between Huddersfield and Barnsley. They throw caution, or whatever else they might have in their hands, to the winds and embark on the making of a giant pie which is probably the cause of acute indigestion in all the inhabitants. They are just recovering from this when they find a reason for making another pie.

Any excuse will do — a royal baby, or the Repeal of the Corn Laws — because it's the *pie* that counts. But until you can pin it down and anchor it under a good, solid crust of respectability, it remains pie in the sky — and nobody ever got a knife and fork into *that*.

They made a pie — probably the first one — to celebrate the recovery (temporary) of George III from mental illness. The most recent one, in 1964, which weighed six tons, raised money to provide a village hall. (It's about time, perhaps, that they found a good and sufficient

reason to embark on another: perhaps the publication of this book!)

Once the mad, pie-making light is in their eyes they're not easily put off. Nor does failure deter them. The 1928 pie, for instance, got stuck in the oven, but that didn't stop it raising £1,000 for Huddersfield Royal Infirmary. The most disastrous pie of all, however, was the one they made in 1887.

It went bad. If ever a fact was incontrovertible, it was *that*. When a pie which has to be moved by two horses pulling a four-wheeled cart goes bad, there just *can't* be any argument about it. So what do you do with a giant pie that nobody can eat? You can only bury it.

And this is where Yorkshire humour comes into its own. In other counties, perhaps, the pie might have been consigned grimly to the earth by men resolved never to get themselves in such a *stew* — shall I say? — again.

Not so in Denby Dale. With that Yorkshire straightness of face which has ever deceived the foreigner, they gave it a funeral before its interment in Toby Wood (where the smell is still said to linger after nearly a hundred years)

and embarked immediately on its successor, the Resurrection Pie, which was to contain 48 stones of flour, 96 stones of potatoes, a heifer, two calves and two sheep. Furthermore, unlike the dear departed pie, it would be made by the ladies of the village. It would thus be safe from contamination by the hired cooks, from foreign big cities like London and Cleckheaton, who had apparently made such a mess of the first pie.

Traditionally, Denby Dale pies are made bigger every time. The 1964 pie contained the beef of ten bullocks, a ton and a half of spuds, half a ton of flour, five hundredweights of lard and 50 gallons of gravy. It was so big that before the great baking day they held cocktail parties in the pie dish (18ft. long, 6ft. wide, 18ins. deep and weighing a ton and a half) which had travelled partly by canal from wherever it was made. Then it sank (or was it sunk? Either way it was very good for pie-publicity).

I've no knowledge that giant pies were ever made in Guiseley. But why should they be, when Guiseley already has a shrine that draws worshippers from across the world? Even stony-hearted Lancastrians have been known to faint with emotion as they confronted it — Harry Ramsden's — the BIGGEST *fish and chip shop in the world!*

And if, due to some Lancastrian plot, it is no longer the biggest, it is still the most famous. What price your aspidistra now, Gracie?

Surely, in the nostrils of any Yorkshireman worth his salt and vinegar, such a temple to the Great God Gastronomy is more than equal to the mere airport which happens to fall within Yeadon's purlieus!

Talking of Yeadon, I heard in Rawdon about the Yeadon councillor who proposed a gondola as an embellishment for Yeadon Dam (or Tarn, as it's called on Sundays). And about the other Yeadon councillor who said, 'Why not get *two* gondolas, Mr. Chairman, an' then we can breed from 'em?'

Guiseley, birthplace of Sooty and once home to an amazing collection of characters who gloried in such names as Bandy Jack, Mothballs and Jack Quack, *alias* Cuckoo (who wandered about the village doing bird imitations), always considered itself intellectually superior to neighbouring Yeadon or it would hardly have

called the latter 'Dozytown' — on politer occasions that is.

Certainly Guiseley folk were not slow in business matters, though it would be wrong to conclude that they were so hard-headed that they were dead to the tenderer emotions.

I am told it was a Guiseley woollen manufacturer who, on his deathbed, received the three sons, partners now, in the company he had developed from one upstairs handloom. The old man's sight was dim, his hearing almost gone. From the windows of the stone house he had built he could no longer enjoy his favourite view — the smoking mill chimney. Clearly the end was near.

'Is that thee, Joe?' whispered the old cracked voice, as one son entered.

'Aye, Father,' replied Joe, his voice choked with emotion.

'Is our Willie there?'

'Aye, an' our Sam an' all. We're all 'ere, Dad — don't upset thiself'. Joe's words were almost stifled by a sob.

Suddenly the old man sat bolt upright. His eyes blazed and in a voice which had regained all its old bull-like roar he demanded:

'Then 'oo the bloody 'ell's lookin' after t' mill?'

A Scotsman's secret!

Guiseley may look down on Yeadon, but Yeadon has certainly one thing that Guiseley lacks... If you want to know what the Scotsman has under his kilt, come to Yeadon! Mind you, that's only one of the reasons for visiting this township, all twists, and turns, on the fringe of Wharfedale.

Yeadon is best known, of course, for the Leeds/Bradford Airport. But contrasting sharply with such modernity are quaintly named streets like World's End, Whackhouse Lane, Calcutta and Football — that's right, Football.

Not far from Football is Marshall Street, where you can find Roger Brayshaw, whose stock-in-trade is jokes — hundreds of them, like Bubbling Boys, Centipedes (Large Wriggling), Dirty Fidos and/or Pussies, Fang Teeth, Flies (Giant), Nail-Through-Finger jokes (Makes People Cringe), Monsters innumerable and, of course, the Scotsman with his kilt.

I won't pretend that Roger and his jokes represent a traditional industry in Yeadon. Nevertheless, there are aspects of his business which are typical both of the adaptability and the earthy humour of the township.

When I visited the fun factory, some of the staff were blowing glass bubbles for Pong Bombs. Charming and immaculate ladies who would be pained by muddy boots on their carpet were matter-of-factly rolling out another popular product for the sort of customer whose delight it is to see Rats, Squashed (large rubber) or Magic Soot where such things ought not to be. And despite the pong from the bombs, they all looked remarkably happy.

Roger couldn't pinpoint a particular best-selling line — they were all good sellers, whether home-produced or imported — like the Toilet Squirts from Germany. But jokey geniuses are constantly thinking up new ideas — or new angles on old ones — whether it's black face soap, non-strike matches or blood nose drops.

Is Roger himself a natural practical joker who enjoys testing his own products? 'Oh, hell, aye!' he grins with relish. 'We try 'em on the women!' Since I've always believed that women secretly enjoy living dangerously, I know now why Roger's staff looked so happy — they get all the thrills of simulated peril with none of the disadvantages of the real thing.

Rogues and idiots!

You may wonder why, according to its neighbours, every town and village in Yorkshire is overflowing with rogues and idiots. James VI of Scotland and I of England (or perhaps, as some say, Robert the Bruce) was apparently to blame for much of the roguery.

This takes us almost into the realms of theology, for if Yorkshire was not the original garden of Eden, the difference was at one time so small as to be hardly noticeable. The only wrong note in those harmonious days was caused by the frequent depredations of Scottish raiders, but even they might have remained a minor irritation had it not been for the message sent over the Border requesting 500 pairs of brogues.

Whether the message was sent by King James on his way through Yorkshire to his coronation in London or by footsore raiding Scots to King Bruce is not important. What matters is that the message was garbled in transmission and reached Scotland as a requisition for 500 pairs of *rogues*.

At least, they *say* it was garbled.

My own theory is that brogues in Scotland were in short supply just then, while rogues were as plentiful there as they have ever been in Lancashire. With a cannyness worthy of Yatton itself, Robert the Bruce (or whoever received the message) saved himself the cost of a large amount of footwear and at the same time was able to rid the country of 1,000 undesirables. Yorkshire has never been the same since.

Can you insult a Yorkshireman?

He sat next to me in a somewhat superior barber's. 'They tell me this is t' place where yer can get a bloody good haircut, so Ah've coom all t'way from bloody Bradford,' he told the hairdresser. So if it isn't a good un Ah'll give you a right bloody rollackin'!'

'Who *told* yer to come?' asked the barber calmly, without looking up from his clipping . . . 'Oh, *'im*! Ah pay *him* £3 for every daft bugger he sends here'.

I doubt if it would have happened quite like that anywhere but in Yorkshire. A straight-faced performance embarked upon spontaneously by both men and all with perfect good humour. (Not to mention that reticence and good taste which have always distinguished the Yorkshireman's polite conversation.)

Done purely and simply for fun, it brightened a visit to the barber's for everybody in the shop — and helps to prove my point that nobody laughs at the Yorkshireman more than he does himself, perhaps because every Yorkshireman is a natural born comedian!

This ability to laugh at ourselves was thoroughly put to the test during a Leeds firm's annual outing to Bridlington.

Having arrived at the seaside a party embarked on a sea-fishing trip, but, being landsmen, they did *not* all enjoy it! It was not long, in fact, before one poor sufferer, Fred by name, surrendered his dentures to Neptune (who rather ungratefully continued to rock the boat as much as ever).

Fortunately, your true Yorkshireman has never been slow to make light of another's suffering. So, surreptitiously, Fred's friend Harry — always ready for a bit of a cod — attached his own dentures to his hook, lowered them gently over the side, then reeled them in a moment later and expressed loud astonishment at his miraculous catch.

'Hey, Fred' said Harry, 'Ah've *copped thi teeth!* Would yer believe it?'

Fred was willing to believe it, but not to care about it overmuch at that moment. Lanquidly he took the teeth

from Harry's hand and put them in his mouth. Then, despair deepening on his features, he took them out.

'*These* in't mine', he said simply — and dropped them in the sea.

If Yorkshiremen really do laugh at themselves there were surely two toothless grins on the homeward bus that night.

When one Yorkshireman, after his first visit to Switzerland, said he could see nowt o' t' scenery for t'bloody hills, he didn't really mean it! But because he said it with a straight face, an outsider might have made the mistake of thinking he did.

Yorkshiremen tend to laugh at the respectably serious gone wrong — like misapplied logic. The farm lad who was found trying his cap on the turnips was being perfectly logical. After all, the farmer had told him to 'find one about as big as thi 'ead', so what more sensible way to go about it?

And at some time during its history, every brass band in Yorkshire, returning late at night after

victory in some contest must have marched itself home from the station with *See the conquering hero comes* — having first removed its boots so as not to disturb the populace.

Dryness, too, and plain speaking are among the essential ingredients of Yorkshire stories — as in this one, where those two qualities combine with the logic.

'Do stop beating that poor donkey, Wilson', said a tender-hearted vicar to one of his flock. 'Don't you know that our Lord rode into Jerusalem on an ass?'

'If it wor this lazy bugger,' said Wilson ''e wouldn't 'ave got theer yet!'

But perhaps the most necessary ingredient of all is understatement. And the classic example of that is provided by George who, on calling to see Albert, his bosom friend of many years, was met at the door by Albert's tearful widow. Between sobs she told him that the long companionship had been ended at last by a call from the Angel of Death.

For a time George was nonplussed . . . But *only* for a time. Then he regained his composure. In the delicate tones demanded by the situation he said, 'Before 'e went — did 'e - er - did 'e say owt abaht a pot o' paint?'

Once you start analysing Yorkshire jokes you are constantly finding such elements which, while not unique to the Broad Acres, are at least characteristic.

But while we certainly *have* our own peculiar brand of fun, it is *not* so peculiar that nobody else can enjoy it. On

the contrary, the popularity of Yorkshire comedians is evidence that our jokes tickle the susceptibilities of most people, provided they have a sufficiently well developed funny bone and understand enough of the language.

Strangely enough, Yorkshiremen *as a race* (the fifth race, someone said, who share these islands with the English, Scots, Welsh and Irish) have not won renown as comics, but rather as villains, or 'tykes', a term which goes back to the 14th century, when it was hardly considered a compliment. Fortunately, Yorkshiremen thrive on insults, even insults such as you'll find in the so-called Yorkshireman's coat of arms depicting a flea, a fly, a magpie and a bacon flitch, with these attendant lines:

> *A flea will bite who ivver it can,*
> *An' soa, my lads, will a Yorkshireman.*
> *A fly will sup wi Dick, Tom or Dan,*
> *An' soa by gow, 'ull a Yorkshireman.*
> *A magpie can talk for a terrible span,*
> *An' soa an' all can a Yorkshireman.*
> *A flitch, is noa gooid till it's hung, you'll agree.*
> *No more is a Yorkshireman, don't you see?*

What a diabolical libel! In any other county, I venture to suggest, this piece of execrable doggerel would have been dismissed with the icy disdain it deserves and would long ago have died of neglect. But you *can't* insult a Yorkshireman, and here it pops up as indefatigably and infuriatingly as the flea mentioned in the first line.

What, in fact, are we saying when we repeat it? That Yorkshiremen are spongers and chatterers who will enrich themselves at anybody's expense and are no good until they are hung?

Surely we all know that the opposite is the case — a more generous, upright and generally admirable set of chaps you'll not find in any other county. If you doubt it, just ask us! Not that we'd ever admit it, but the vehemence with which we deny it is surely, in its way, an admission!

There are those who say the Yorkshireman's coat of arms, and its explanatory verse were devised by an envious foreigner. Granted that non-Yorkshiremen *are* invariably envious (no matter how they try to conceal the fact beneath a facade of contempt or criticism), I beg leave to doubt this theory: there is something in the rhythm and the aptly used dialect phrases of the verse that bespeaks the tyke.

So if a Yorkshireman composed it, what sort of a renegade bounder was he, we ask ourselves, thus to heap infamy upon his fellows? What could have induced him to do it?

I give you the explanation in one word — modesty! Outsiders may mock and scoff and undoubtedly they will, but what other explanation can there be?

The same sort of modesty inspired the author (perhaps it was even the same Yorkshireman) who concocted the rather better-known 'Yorkshire motto'. Somewhat hesitantly I must inform you that my wife presented me with a mug bearing precisely this piece of regional self-denigration. Did she, I wondered anxiously, *mean* anything by it? Perish the thought! Who would thus impugn the generosity of a chap like me? (I know — don't tell me — obviously my wife would.) If you haven't already guessed, here's how it goes:

> *Hear all, see all, say nowt,*
> *Eat all, sup all pay nowt*
> *An' if tha ivver does*
> > *Owt for nowt*
> *Allus do it for thissen*

Well, obviously, nobody would say things like that about himself and mean them. So I repeat — it's just another example of that native modesty of ours. Dazzled by the splendour of our own supreme good character we just have to pretend there are a few flaws somewhere. If we tend to overdo it, that's entirely due to our well known thoroughness.

Yorkshiremen, after all, have plenty to be modest about. And that's no small claim to make — if you think about it.

A Glorious Company

The fact that Yorkshire is the biggest county should hardly need saying — but you know how ignorant foreigners can be!

I wouldn't mention this matter of mere vulgar size if people were not so impressed by it. But while I'm at it, here are a few more assorted vulgar superlatives:

We shall soon have the world's longest single span suspension bridge — over the Humber. (And forget all that nonsense about Humberside — Hessle, to a Yorkshireman, remains in Yorkshire.)

At Redcar (again still in Yorkshire so far as this book is concerned) we still have the oldest lifeboat in the world (no longer in use, I might add).

At Middleton Railway, Leeds, the first rack railway in the world was converted from a wooden wagonway opened in 1758. Still on railways — the highest main line railway summit in Britain (1,167ft.) is attained on the Settle-Carlisle line; while much of the coal which once powered the locomotives using it came from England's largest single coalfield, in South Yorkshire.

Most of all, we have Yorkshiremen themselves, and what a glorious if motley company they are!

Captain Cook was a Yorkshireman, born in that part of the county then called Cleveland. (It still is, though today Cleveland has become the name of a so-called 'New County'. I wonder what the old circumnavigator would have said about that!)

Joseph Priestley, the discoverer of oxygen, was not only one of the greatest scientists but, like all good Yorkshiremen, a bit of a wag. While he was living in Leeds a local woman who considered him a miracle worker asked him to exorcise her demon. Obligingly he gave her such a shock with one of his electrical machines that she was immediately cured!

Guy Fawkes, too, you might say was a bit of a practical joker in his way, but his greatest joke of all fell rather flat! Guy had hoped that it would be Parliament that fell flat — and how many since then (and not only Yorkshiremen) have thought there was something to be said for the idea?

Jonathan Martin who, like Guy, lived in York was also a man of decided views. Since his own religious opinions

were somewhat at variance with those of the Anglican Church, he tried to prove his point by burning down York Minster and almost succeeded! (But you can read all about that in a book called *Queer Folk* — or have I mentioned that before?)

Jack Metcalf (Blind Jack of Knaresborough), the famous roadmaker, and one of the most remarkable men to have lived in Yorkshire or anywhere else, must have had a sense of humour as big as his own stalwart frame or he would never have survived the vicissitudes that began when he went blind at the age of six after an attack of smallpox. But blindness didn't stop him serving in the British Army during the Forty-five rebellion, or eloping with his sweetheart, Dolly Benson, the night before she was to marry another man.

Sir George Cayley, born at Scarborough, in 1773, was squire of Brompton and Yorkshire's own aeronautical genius. But he possessed his proper share of Yorkshire caution, and when in 1852 he launched a revolutionary glider of his own design, he launched his coachman, too, as passenger!

Surprisingly, the pioneer flyer failed to appreciate the honour. 'You 'ired me to drive, Squire,' stammered the poor terrified man, on his return to earth, 'n-not to fly. Ah-Ah'm givin' yer mi noatice!'

Then, nearer our own time, there was Percy Shaw.

Some said Percy was eccentric, but if he was, we could do with more of Percy's brand of eccentricity (though I would prefer to call it genius).

On foggy nights Percy would find his way to his Halifax home guided by the reflection of his headlights on the tramlines. But tramlines have a habit of being taken up and *then* what do you do?

Percy thought about it. He'd always been 'summat of a nackler' and the idea he nackled next provided him with just about the most far-flung memorial even a Yorkshireman could hope for: he invented the 'Catseyes' road stud, for which motorists by the million have blessed him — or if not, they ought to have done.

Percy saw a problem and solved it . . . And so did Joe Jagger, though in Joe's case the problem was rather different: how to break the bank at Monte Carlo!

Joseph Hobson Jagger, born at Shelf, near Bradford, was, like Percy, a bit of a 'nackler', a mill engineer whose professional interest was captured during a holiday visit to Monte Carlo by the roulette wheels in the Casino.

'Bit of a rough job', he probably told himself, having examined the finish of the cylinders. 'Wouldn't do in Bradford at all!' And he felt certain that in such circumstances Lady Luck hardly had as free a hand as she ought to have. With the help of spectators he put his theory to the test and discovered that — yes — the wheels at certain tables had a tendency to favour particular numbers!

'We're on to summat 'ere, owd lad', said Joe to himself, and he began to play the tables himself, winning several thousand francs on the very first night.

Naturally the Casino officials were suspicious about the success of the 'Lucky Englishman', as they called him (not knowing that he was really from Shelf). They ordered their security men to keep him under observation. But Joe wasn't daft and he soon saw what they were up to. He made sure he didn't always win, which foxed them even more. How *did* he do it, they wondered. He certainly wasn't operating any of the 40 'winning systems' that were known to the Casino authorities.

On the second night Joe collected even more winnings — but this time all from the same wheel. Very well, said the management, we'll change the wheel. And on the third night they waited, no doubt confidently, to see Joseph Hobson Jagger, mill engineer from Shelf, come a cropper.

Again Joe outsmarted them. He had somehow anticipated that move and secretly marked the winning cylinder. Now he simply walked to the table where it was and calmly began to play. His pile reached the largest amount ever won at Monte Carlo by a single player — £400,000.

But the Casino management was no more stupid than Joe. (Well perhaps a bit more, because he, after all, was a mill engineer from Shelf.) They had noticed his move to the new table, and at last it dawned on them that the factor in Joe's success was the cylinder. When they replaced it with a new one, Joe knew the game was up and never again, so far as I know, entered the Casino.

He came home to Shelf and proved that even the cleverest men make mistakes. He gave up his job at t'mill, bought a big house and spent the rest of his life in luxury and — say some — in misery because he couldn't find enough to do.

Perhaps he'd have been happier if he'd never won all that brass!

We could go on — and on — about Yorkshiremen and their homeland: about York Minster, largest medieval Gothic church in Europe; about Yorkshire's claim to have more inns than any other county, one of them, at Tan Hill, being the highest in England, though now, by a whisker it lies within Durham's extended boundaries. Need I tell you that morally, at least, it remains in Yorkshire? (Some dark night we must put it back quietly where it belongs — on our side of the imaginary line which some Whitehall bureautic considers an adequate substitute for the River Tees. It's only a few yards and what's that to a determined Yorkshireman or two?)

But *need* I go on? Yorkshiremen know they live in the greatest place in the world and it's their bounden duty to enlighten the rest of the world about it, though southerners and — sad to say — Lancastrians seem strangely determined to remain ignorant.

Never mind, this book will no doubt enlighten them — once they've learnt to read . . .

The Happy Heart of Cricket

When demob was looming and Harry East could hardly wait to return to Bradford, cricket and all things lovely, he wrote to Bingley Cricket Club offering his skill, and his letter, roughly translated, ran thus:

'I was nobbut just good enough five years since: I shall be worse now, and I've no intention of practising'.

Bingley C.C. noted the warning but made him captain of the Second XI. After all, they were Yorkshiremen, just like Harry, and they appreciated frankness.

His reason for choosing Bingley? 'Stephen' (his son) 'was a little lad then, and there's nowt more boring for a little lad than watching his Dad play cricket. Bingley ground was near the riverside and meadows, where a child could amuse himself.'

No child of Harry's, you gather, would ever be a 'cricket orphan', any more than his wife, Kathleen, would be a cricket widow. Nowadays the Easts like to watch cricket, not only at Lord's now and then ('it's a nice ride out') but at Northowram, Halifax. There are two adjacent grounds there, you see, and you can walk through a gate from one to t' other. Kathleen likes that. 'She gets a choice of teas', Harry explains.

But back to Bingley, which not only saw Harry's double triumph in the Priestley Shield, but his exit from active participation in the game. Some cricketers never know when to stop, says Harry, who feels he was somewhat helped — by fate and the Priestley Shield — to choose his own moment of exit.

'Have you *seen* t' Priestley Shield?' he says. 'It weighs a ton! We'd won it the year before and then we had to lug the blessed thing all t' way back to Saltaire to play for it again.

'Anyway, we won again, and this great thing was presented back to me after t' match. I handed it to the next chap *right* sharp, and he passed it to the next. It went down the line until it finished up in the hands of a committee man.

"'What do you want me to do wi' this, Harry?'" he said.

'Chuck it in t' bloody river', said Harry. 'We were at Saltaire after all. I was more or less ready to finish but I've a feeling that episode helped me on mi way . . .'

To Harry, as you may have gathered, cricket is for playing, and I think he was a bit surprised that I should want to interview him about his career in the game. 'I've never been owt better than a Sunday school cricketer,' he half-apologised.

I'm not so sure. In case you don't know, Harry is a comic (and sometimes a serious) writer of no mean talent; he is a popular cricket raconteur and now, in semi-retirement, the headmaster of a small independent school in Halifax. He is also (glory be to the West Riding) a Senior Examiner in Textile Calculations (City and Guilds of London Institute).

But it was Harry the one-time cricketer who concerned me. A book on Yorkshire laughter *must* include cricket, but what sort of cricket? Harry says it isn't the big name players who keep cricket going. It's friends of his like Clifford Sykes and Percy Hardacre.

Clifford has at one time or another won the Bradford League, Huddersfield League and Central Yorkshire batting averages. He was president of the Yorkshire Council and coach at Silcoates School. 'He helps look after the Central Yorkshire League's representative teams, umpires on Saturday afternoons if they are a man short, and he was playing in good class league cricket until he was over 50.'

A new season began and Clifford thought he'd have his eyes tested. 'Do you wear bi-focals?' asked the optician, 'I don't wear glasses at all,' said Clifford.

Percy Hardacre, secretary of West Bradford League and gigantic at least in his dedication, resigned eight times at as many annual meetings but always chose a moment when mass deafness had apparently descended on the meeting.

'He was secretary of Ingrow St. John's at the same time and twice to my knowledge they've lost their ground and he's found them a new 'un — and practically made it into a cricket field by himself. Every Saturday he rolls the wicket, marks it out and lights the boilers for the women.

'He's in his middle 70s, but if they knock a ball into the River Worth he still fetches it out. And after the match he rolls the wicket again. It's chaps like *him* who mean a lot to cricket,' says Harry reverently. 'They're barmy in one sense...' Here beats the authentic, happy heart of cricket.

To know how Harry got into such a select company you have to know a little about his background. His parents were Pennine Victorians, 'puritanical but not hard', says Harry, whose mother waged a continuous fight to get her husband into her beloved chapel. Unfortunately he usually had a more pressing engagement at his equally beloved Working Men's Club. To quote one of Harry's articles in *Yorkshire Life* 'My mother was a chapel-going woman... and although she might have had some doubts as to the object of this mortal span, of one thing she was certain — it was not for pleasure'.

And there, she and Harry were completely at variance, for his early life, on his own admission, was spent largely in pursuit of that very thing, pleasure, whether at dance halls, the pictures, or, if necessary, the cricket field.

But in those days parents were equal to their children. When Harry was suspected of breaking the family rule by going dancing on a weekday, on the pretence of playing billiards for the Congregational chapel against the Methodists, his father, whose role was apparently that of family umpire, calmly burnt Harry's dancing slippers before his eyes.

Then, judicially, he turned to Harry. 'Of course, lad,' he said, 'I've no proof of anything. But if you want to go dancing next Saturday you'll have to go in your clogs.'

Harry's Dad was a plumber. Once, a relation had delivered some glass, which was a heavy job, deserving the customary tanner honorarium. *'Nay'*, he said, with family feeling affronted, *'Ah dooan't want that'*.

'Tak' it!' ordered Harry's Dad, and when the tanner was refused again, he flung it into the cab of his relative's lorry and declared: 'Tha'rt no relation o' mine till five o'clock!'

Such, then, were Harry's parents and as so often happened with well brought-up youths, he went from crisis to crisis, getting locked out of the Marlborough Rooms on the bitterly cold February night of the Master Plumbers' Ball — while his coat was locked in. And on a warmer occasion sweating in fear of a murder charge after catching the truculent proprietor of a coconut shy nicely between the eyes with his own ball.

But it was the misdoings of others — or so he was told — that got Harry involved with Sunday school cricket. The teenage team had won themselves a bad reputation by such crimes as singing bawdy songs while travelling through Bradford on the open front of a tram. 'After that they had to have a chapel worthy with them whenever they went to a match'. That gent took Harry along as a very young scorer. And that is how he became a fund of cricketing stories — 'and they're all true.' Like the one about the bowler who sometimes found himself put on to bowl all through the innings while at other matches he never bowled a ball.

Asked to explain, the captain said, 'I put thee on to bowl on a cold day, because tha'rt t' only chap in t' team who can afford a sweater. When tha'rt bowlin', *I* wear thy sweater'. (In those days, says Harry, bowlers weren't soft, putting their sweaters back on after every over!)

Harry courted a lass whose father was on the committee at Bingley. After a while her father asked Harry's intentions. They were apparently honourable, if a bit unhurried.

'Well, as soon as tha weds her', said the girl's father, 'Ah'll see tha gets into t' first team at Bingley'.

* * * * *

At Ingrow, near Keighley, the River Worth carves out a deep valley. Ingrow cricket field at the top of a hill looks in one direction towards the hills of Haworth and, in another, over to Ilkley Moor, while almost beneath your feet you see the mills of Keighley.

Sometimes, says Harry, Brontë pilgrims fetch up at Ingrow by mistake. It was one such, an American 'with a

cigar a mile long, field glasses like Kew Observatory and a backside like a Lancashire boiler', who looked around with interest and then addressed an ancient local thus:

'Ah, rural and industrial!'

'Tha what?' said the local, not stirring from his seat: 'Rural and industrial', said the American in a louder voice. The ancient pondered. 'Tha must be in t' wrong field', he said at last. 'It's Ingrow and Denholme that's laikin' 'ere today'.

At Silsden, said Harry, they had the best team in the Airedale and Wharfedale league. But one day they lost by nine wickets and an old man in the crowd had no doubts about the reason.

'*That's* what's to blame', he told Harry, pointing to a nearby school. 'When I was a lad we laiked cricket every afternoon in summer till goin' 'ome time. That lot goes out one hawf day a week. What are they *doin'*?'

''Appen', ventured Harry, ''appen they're teaching 'em to read an' write.'

The old man looked at him astonished: 'What the 'ell does anybody in Silsden want to read an' write for?'

Where would local cricket be without the classic utterances of old men. At a village charity match where the Round Table were thrashing the Amateur Dramatic

Society, Harry heard one of them say to his wife: 'Tha sees that fielder? He was Aladdin in that pantomime we saw last Christmas . . . If I were in his shoon I'd be rubbin' me lamp like bloody hell now!'

In a cup-tie at Salts, in the days when umpires were paid for two nights only, the game was in its second night and darkness was falling fast. But when the batsmen appealed against bad light, the umpires insisted, 'Carry on'.

One batsman asked that the sight board be moved.

'Right or left?' he was asked.

'Nearer,' said the batsman. 'Ah can't see the bloody thing.'

Harry respects umpires, whom he considers admirably unbiased and conscientious. But that is not to say they are of unmixed quality! Two second teams were competing in the bottom division of one Industrial League, than which,

I gather, nothing in cricket was lower. After the match, one captain, shocked to his rock-bottom soul, addressed an umpire thus:

'*Tha*', he said, 'Art a *bloody — rotten —* umpire!'

'Ah know I am', said the umpire. 'If Ah were any good, would they appoint me to umpire two such rotten teams as yours?'

Sad to say, war catches up even with cricket. Harry was playing for Bingley against Eccleshill in a Priestley Cup tie of 1941. The following week he was to go into the army. 'There's not much brass in the army', he told Kathleen, seeing a chance to enrich himself.

He bowled out two of the enemy with successive balls. And the prospect of a hat trick moved Manny Martindale, the West Indian professional, to offer advice: 'Whatever you do, bowl a straight one, Harry'.

Perhaps the tension was too much, but Harry's next ball was 'a right high donkey drop. It bent in the air and the batsman was out l.b.w.

'I got a bagful of brass to take into the army', said Harry, 'and in those days a hat-trick was rewarded with the ball mounted on silver wickets.'

'Well done, Harry, lad', said a committee man. 'First leave yer get, we'll present yer wi' this ball'. 'I'm still waiting for it', says Harry, 'after nearly 40 years.'

In a time-limit match against Keighley, Bingley had half an hour to play, and Harry's instructions as he strode to the crease were to 'Get 'im 'it!'

Facing a South African test match bowler, Harry played not a single decent stroke, 'yet the score board was racing round. I wasn't bowled out and as we were going off, this South African beckoned me to him'.

'The trouble with you, young man,' he said with ill-concealed fury, 'is that you can't bat *well enough* to be got out!'

When Harry played cricket, the clubs he knew existed in a constant state of poverty. Once when he had reached 48 a player panted to the wicket bearing 'a very important message from t' captain'. Harry, impressed, awaited some vital instruction on tactics.

'He says,' said the messenger, having recovered his breath,' he says if tha gets thi 50, he 'asn't enough in t'kitty to pay thi thi talent brass.'

An equally desperate message was delivered by a Riddlesden captain's son when, after a miserable season the team were in sight of a league batting record.

Said the little lad from the tea tent, 'She wants to know when tha'rt bahn to declare'. He was shooed back to the tent but returned almost immediately.

'If tha *doesn't* declare in five minutes,' he told the captain, 'she's bahn to mash t' tea an' it's bahn to be cowd!' Close and Boycott know absolutely nothing of such problems . . .

In the army Harry had what he calls a right cushy billet as research statistician to the consultant army psychiatrist working at a War Office School of Infantry — 'Aptitude testing and all that'.

One day there arrived a new C.O. — 'a real fire-eating brass hat, but with no authority over me', says Harry. 'Tell me, sergeant', the C.O. said, 'what exactly do you *do* here?'

'I wasn't right certain', said Harry, 'but I tried to explain.'

'Sergeant,' said the brass-hat, after a pause for thought, 'it's men like you make me bleed from the gut downwards.'

'That was Saturday,' said Harry, 'the next day, Sunday, I played cricket for the unit and got 80 or 90. I cracked one against the pavilion that nearly knocked his red hat off'.

'Sergeant', said the brass-hat after the match, 'you may stay here as long as you like, but just keep out of my bloody way from Monday morning till Sunday lunchtime!'

Cricket humour, says Harry, is unconscious humour. Seeing the scoring tins laid out in serried ranks reading 13579, Kathleen said, 'They *have* got a lot of runs, Harry.'

That was at Haworth. The Methodists were batting, and they were always a methodical lot.

Figures can deceive as well in cricket as elsewhere. One pro in the Bradford League had had a rotten season — batting average 6, bowling average 79. Sacked, he applied for a job in the Lancashire League, reversing the figures, and was appointed by a club who felt certain they had signed a match winner. It took them two seasons to discover their error — but that, of course, was in Lancashire . . .

Even Harry can be serious at times. He says cricket provided his philosophy for life — which seems a good note to end on.

'I was only a bit of a lad, playing for Bingley against Spen — a derby match. They had scored 180 and we were 70 for 9. I was batting when Bert, an old pro, joined me and we'd half an hour to play to make a draw of it.

'I've never seen *anyone* bend the laws of cricket like he did! He moved the sight board, changed his bat and did everything he could to play for time. I don't think he batted for half of the time, but we made a draw of it.

'The Spen supporters thought we'd cheated them of a certain victory. They hooted, catcalled and did everything but throw bricks at us. "Tha taks no notice o' that," instructed Bert.

'But the Bingley supporters made two lines and clapped and cheered us all the way back to the pavilion. It might have gone to my young head, but as we walked back, side by side, Bert gave me another sideways look — "An, think on," he said, "tha taks even *less* notice o' *that!*"'

Hamlet, or t' Prince o' Lupset

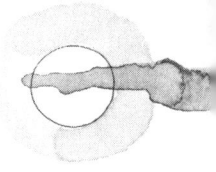

by Bill Tykespeare, the deservedly lesser-known Yorkshire poet

    At Elsinore Palace, one cold winter's neet,
    Sentries stood around frozen to deeath,
    When all of a sudden they got such a freet,
    It fair left 'em gaspin' for breeath!

'It's a ghooast!' says one chap. 'Gerraway!' says 'is mate,
    'Ah dunnot believe such a tale.
    Ah suggest it's more probably summat tha ate
    As didn't agree wi' thi ale.'

'It's clankin' its chains', said the first — 'can't tha see? —
    On its armour o' best Sheffield steel.
    An' groanin' wi' anguish an' pain! Seems to me
    'At that phantom is noan varry weel!'

'It's t'owd King', t'other said, 'there's no doubt in my mind
    Cos Ah allus remember a face.
    Go run round the palace an' see 'f tha can find
    Young 'Amlet — 'e's somewheer in t'place'.

Well, 'Amlet was fair ta'en aback, you can guess —
    'It's mi Dad', 'e said, 'no doubt o' that.
    Ah'll admit he looks skinny an' rayther a mess,
    But then — 'e wor niver reight fat.

'Speyk, Father, speyk, 'ast a message for me?'
    Said the young prince, impatient an' hasty,
    'If tha *'asn't,* Ah'd better be off for mi tea —
    Cos the Queen's cookin' summat reight tasty'.

T'ghost groaned again, 'twas a terrible din:
    'Shut thi clack 'oil, an' listen', it said.
    'Twas thy own uncle, Claudius, 'oo didded me in,
    An' Ah shan't 'ave no peace till 'e's dead.

'Yer see, Ah was killed by mi very own brother —
A right mucky trick, yer must own,
An' then t'cheeky pup went an' married yer mother,
An' set 'isself up on *my* throne!'

'Ah'll avenge thee, dear Father, reight quick', 'Amlet said.
'But first Ah'll on Claudius spy,
An' to fooil 'im, Ah'll try to act daft in the 'ead' —
Said 'is Dad, 'Nay, tha's no need to try!'

Now 'Amlet, till then, had been courtin' a lass
Called Ophelia, a grand bit o' knittin'.
But since he took queer, he ne'er once made a pass —
Which Ophelia 'ardly felt fittin'!

Well, 'Amlet 'isself knew 'e warn't doin' right
By the lass, so he wrote 'er a letter —
'Twas full o' strange notions revealin' 'is state,
So Ophelia did not feel much better!

She went to 'er Dad — old Polonius was 'e —
T'new King's right-hand man, full of guile.
She said, 'Sitha, Dad, 'Amlet's written to me —
An' Ah can't say Ah'm struck with 'is style!'

So Polonius this letter showed unto the King,
Sayin' 'What dosta think o' this, Guv?'
But Claudius poo-poohed it — 'A triflin' thing,'
He said, 'Amlet's nobbut in love!'

'Amlet sent for some mummers to put on a play,
Containin' a murder most 'orrid.
It made the King act in a strange, guilty way
An' 'e went to bed clutchin' is fore'ead

Said the King to 'is missus, 'Tak' t' lad on one side
An' see'f tha can mak' 'im see sense.
Ah'll put up wi' a lot, but a King 'as 'is pride
Ah'm fair stalled with 'is himpertinence!'

But 'Amlet refused to take 'eed of 'is Mum,
Sayin' 'No, Ma, thee listen to me.
An' mak' no attempt to run off, cos, by gum,
Ah've some 'arsh words to say unto thee!'

Then 'e grabbed 'er an' made 'er sit down — where she stood!
And rebuked 'er in tones stern an' bitter.
'E said, 'Mend thi ways, Mother, try to be good —'
So she skriked, 'cos she thought 'e wo'd 'it 'er!

Now Polonius, who'd 'idden 'issen in the room,
Feared this would the Queen much embarrass.
'E yelled, *'Help the Queen!'* in a voice full of doom —
An' got stabbed by the Prince through the arras*.

It means a tapestry — honest!

'A right bloody deed, 'Amlet, lad', said 'is Mum,
   'Tha're in it now — up to thi neck!'
'But not 'alf as bloody as *thy* deed, by gum!'
   Said the Prince — adding, 'Ee, flippin' 'eck!'

For the ghost of 'is Dad had appeared once again.
   It said, ''Amlet, mi patience wears thin.
Tha said tha'd avenge me — Ah'm wonderin' when
   Tha'll start framin' thiself to begin!'

Now Polonius' death made the King rather vexed.
   He said, 'This time the lad's got to go.
Ah'm sure 'e's gone crackers! What *will* 'e do next?'
   An' the Queen answered, 'Nay, I don't know.'

'We'll send 'im to England', the King said, *'that* way
   'E might get away with 'is crime.
They're *all* mad in England — at least, so they say'.
   So he booked t'lad a seat in quick time.

In England he meant to 'ave 'Amlet done in,
But a pirate crew captured his ship.
Skipper said, "E's a king's son — we might get run in',
So they dropped 'im off after t' next trip.

'E got 'ome to find that Ophelia was dead:
It 'ad been such a strain on her brain.
They'd a buffet at t'funeral, with 'am and brown bread.
An' *some* greedy pigs went round again!

Then 'er grief-stricken brother, Laertes by name,
Jumped into 'er grave with a yell.
So 'Amlet, not wishin' to be put to shame,
Landed smack on 'er coffin 'issel'!

This led to a scrap — an unseemly affair, which the
King said was quite a disgrace.
'Nay, nay, lads! Coom, coom', he said, 'do 'ave a care,
This is neether the time nor the place.'

The King said, 'A fencin' match I will arrange
To show all ill-feeling is gone.'
(An' in case at a funeral that strikes you as strange,
'Ang on a bit — it might catch on!)

Ophelia's brother a mucky trick played —
It rebounded on 'im (sarves 'im reight!).
To steal an advantage he poisoned 'is blade...
But by so doin' sealed 'is own fate!

In the *mêlée* poor 'Amlet was mortally stabbed,
But before he knew what 'ad befell,
'Avin' dropped 'is own weapon, Laertes' 'e grabbed
An' fatally stabbed 'im, as well!

Came a shriek from the Queen — not inspired by fun! —
As she spat out a mouthful o' tea.
'Ah think tha's supped summat tha s'udn't 'ave done,'
Said the King. 'That's for *'Amlet* — not thee!'

As 'is mother fell dead at 'is feet, there an' then,
'Amlet said, 'Summat's wrong, Ah can see'.
And L*a*ertes replied, 'Tha can say that again!
Dosta know that we're all bahn to dee?'

''Appen so', 'Amlet said, 'but Ah'll tell thi one thing' —
An' 'e took t' poisoned sword in 'is 'and —
If Ah've got to dee Ah'll tak' wi' me yond king,
'Cos Ah've 'ad all of 'im Ah can stand.'

So 'e stabbed 'im — an' slew 'im — an' thus 'e was dead!
An' that's just abaht all there is in it —
'Amlet's dad was avenged . . . Is there more to be said?
There *is!* Thee just 'ang on a minute!

This tale 'as a moral tha'd do well to 'eed —
You might think it's summat an' nowt —
But if *tha* meets a ghoast, move away at top speed
An' above all — DOAN'T PROMISE IT OWT!

Wimmin! Or Sex in Yorkshire

Old Ben had never been much of a man for the women. That, at least, was the general opinion. After all, he'd reached 75 and had neither married nor lived ovver t'brush (which as even southerners may deduce is a bit — but only a bit — like keeping a dog without a licence ... except that they can't fine you for it).

Every night he sat in his favourite corner of the bar, ready to join in conversation — polite or otherwise — about most subjects — barring women, or anything even remotely connected with sex. On such matters he had strictly nowt to contribute. There were those who said that Ben's experience in such fields was limited if not non-existent. Others would remind you that 'still watters ran deep' and that 'quiet uns is allus t' warst'.

'Ah tell thi', declared young Riley, 'he wouldn't reco'nize a naked woman if he fell ovver one'.

'Tak' 'im to t'nudist camp at Low Ghyll an' see', suggested Tom Aykroyd.

'Nay, 'e'd niver go', young Riley replied, 'but' (looking serious for once) 'tha's given me a hidea'.

A few nights later he entered the bar with a mysterious smile on his cheeky young face and a small yellow packet in his hand.

To his boon companions he explained that he had visited the environs of the nudist camp and over the hedge had engaged one of the prettiest of the sun-worshippers in conversation. Not only that, but, succumbing to his impertinent boyish charm, she had even agreed to let him photograph her in graceful pose amongst the hay.

'Coom on — let's 'ave a look . . . *Oooargh!*' Rapturous groanings welcomed the delectable sight.

'Shur*rup!*' warned young Riley. 'Tha're bahn to give t'show away'. He glanced anxiously at Ben but found him nodding in his corner, quite unconcerned by the hubbub.

'Show 'im it!' urged Tom Aykroyd.

'Nay' said the landlord, 'what if 'e 'as an 'eart attack an' dees? 'Ow wilt tha feel then?'

'No worse nor him, Ah dare say', young Riley replied.

''E'll do' is *nut!*' said the landlord.

''E'll niver turn a hair', said Tom.

Young Riley handed the venerable one the photograph. 'Assay, Ben, what does tha think abaht this?'

With infuriating slowness, Ben took another swig at his pint then laid it carefully on the bar. He took the photograph carefully between a leathery thumb and forefinger and placed it upon his knee. Then, from a capacious waistcoat pocket he drew a pair of antique spectacles.

The assembled boozers watched in tense and nerve-racked silence as he slowly picked up the photograph and focussed his dim old eyes upon it. Then —

'By . . . !' he ejaculated 'Ah know what *that* is. Well Ah niver! *Eeh*, who'd 'ave thowt it? By *gow!*'

'Ah *warned* thee it might be too much for 'im', said Tom, on the point of calling an ambulance.

'Ah wish tha'd put t'leet on', said Ben touchily to the landlord. 'Ah'm tryin' to look at this 'ere . . . Coom *on*, let's 'ave some leet!'

Hurriedly the landlord obliged.

'It *is*', declared Ben, still studying the photograph. 'Ah thowt it was and by gum it is!'

'What, Ben', What?' demanded young Riley.

'If that's nooan Joe Hardaker's 'aystack', said Ben, 'Ah'll go to 'ell!'

Sex, as any Yorkshireman will tell you, is what they carry coal in (except that being a Yorkshireman he would say coil — as in coil 'oil).

But don't let that mislead you: the Yorkshireman knows what sex is all right. If he tells you it's the number that comes between five and seven, he's really trying to hide his deeply passionate nature.

You must remember the Yorkshire lad, deeply in love, who almost drove his mother frantic by mooning about the house, unable to think of anything but his beloved, yet apparently quite incapable of doing anything to forward his suit.

'Tha can't go on like this', said his mother. 'Go see t'lass. Ah'm sure tha'll feel a lot better if tha does.'

'Ah *will*, Mother', said the lad, with sudden decision. 'Ah'll go this minute an' see 'er'. He donned his best suit, slicked back his hair and left the house while his mother gazed fondly after him.

An hour later he returned, his face aglow with happiness.

'Well, did yer see her, lad?' asked his mother.

'*See* her? Ah did that!' replied her son. 'If Ah 'adn't bobbed down quick, behind a wall, she'd 'ave seen me an' all!'

Modesty, you see, has always been one of the Yorkshireman's greatest faults. I'm not so sure about Yorkshire *women* if we are to believe all the tales told about our rude Pennine forebears (and I do mean rude).

Talk about permissiveness? An old friend in Holmfirth told me about a game they used to play in his grandfather's time, called *Ringin' in th'Owd Adam Bells*. This happened during laikin' neets (what posh folk down south would call social evenings), during which everyone contributed according to his talents — by singing, fiddling or clog dancing. And by suppin' ale.

Now George's grandad has seen *most* of what happened on Laikin' Neets with his own two een, but *Ringin' in th'Owd Adam Bells* was X-certificate stuff — from which young uns were excluded. If the paper window-blind

hadn't been torn, George's grandad might never have known what happened — and neither would we, for most local historians either didn't know or were too polite to record it.

The women would sit on the floor in a circle facing the men, who formed a circle around *them,* facing inward.

Then, while a fiddler in the centre played a lively tune the women would sing (but don't ask me what they meant by it) —

> *Ring in th'Owd Adam Bells*
> *Kitlins i't'Clough.*
> *Who can see my bare arse?*

After which they would fall backwards, flinging their skirts over their heads, while the men finished the verse —

> *Me, fair enough!*

So much for our Victorian ancestors and their prudish ways! Hardly surprising, was it, that George's questions as to 'what happened next' were not answered (except, perhaps, by a grandfatherly injunction to 'figure it out for thissen').

Such high jinks were purely (well, better say *simply*) for entertainment, because when it came to the serious business of matrimony, a Yorkshireman was no more apt to be swept off his feet by such laikin' neet revelations than he was by a pretty face.

'Nay, lad!' said a Yorkshire father when his son rhapsodised about his beloved's facial charms. 'Nivver 'eed 'er face . . . It's 'er *'ands* tha mun look at when tha'rt after a wife.'

Finding a wife was one thing: getting rid of her was something else again, but here, too, it was a poor sort of Yorkshireman who couldn't make a profit on the deal — in his own eyes at least.

Prices, as you might expect, varied. In 1806 a woman at Knaresborough was sold for sixpence and a quid of tobacco; in which case the vendor did marginally better, perhaps, than the husband at Selby, who disposed of his wife in 1862 from the steps of the market cross for one pint of ale.

Don't feel too sorry for the wives, they sometimes got the best of the bargain. Like that 'clean, industrious, quiet and careful woman, attractive in appearance and well mannered', whose drunken fool of a husband put her up for auction in York in the 1830s, having dragged her to the market by means of a halter.

She was doubtless well rid of him when he let her go — throwing in the halter — for 7s. 6d. Twenty years later, when her husband died, she married the man he had sold her to and lived happily ever after, so if there was a last laugh in the sorry affair, she got it.

Nineteenth-century Yorkshiremen sold their wives in Hull, Pontefract and Sheffield for prices ranging from 4s. to 20 guineas. Nor were Yorkshiremen the only offenders. A Carlisle man exchanged *his* wife for 20s. and a Newfoundland dog.

Mind you, the wife-vendors didn't always make a sale.

'Ah'd *sell* my missus if Ah could find a customer', said a Bradford man one day to his friend.

'Ah'll 'ave 'er', said the friend (who was probably equally drunk). So the bellman was hired to advertise the sale, and the 'merchandise', bedecked in ribbons, was put on show in front of a local beerhouse.

All that was missing was the customer — whose own

wife wouldn't let him out of the house!

In the 1820s Rachel Heap, of Sowerby, near Halifax, heard that her soldier husband was missing, presumed dead, so she 'married' Sam Lumb, by whom she had three children.

Who, then, should reappear, but her first husband, the reports of whose death had been premature, or even grossly exaggerated!

Clearly something had to be done and I'm happy to report that it was all settled very amicably.

'Ah'll buy her off thee', said Sam, who had grown quite attached to Rachel over the years.

'Done!' said her resurrected husband (no spoilsport) and Rachel and Sam, who obviously liked to see things 'done proper', went to the altar yet again, and this time, presumably, for keeps.

Nowadays, even Yorkshiremen rarely expect to make money on disposing of a troublesome spouse. They can, however, be quite accommodating at times.

I greatly admire the aplomb of a friend of a friend, the sort of quiet chap who refuses to be rattled even when his wife makes her periodic threats to leave him.

Mildness itself, he simply says, 'Let me know when you're goin', love, an' I'll give you a lift'.

Oh, Brother Jucundus!

Brother Jucundus, though he lived centuries ago and was a monk — of sorts — was very much a Yorkshire lad and like one or two more of that tribe, fond of his ale.

Doubtless, too, he talked like the Yorkshireman he was — except during the time when he was astonished to find himself observing a vow of silence he had never actually taken . . . And he certainly demonstrated superbly that knack of falling on one's feet that is so much admired in the King of Counties.

But I'm gettin' in front o' meself, as Brother Jucundus himself might have said. Start at t' beginnin' lad, if tha'rt bahn to tell a tale and doan't *yammer on!*

Drink was his problem and what scrapes it got him into both in his secular and his religious life! At York Fair one bibulous day long before he became a monk, he presumably went through the various stages of intoxication in which elation is followed by disillusion and melancholy; whereupon, overcome by a sense of sin, he presented himself at St. Leonard's Priory, which stood next to St. Mary's Abbey in that same city of York. Indeed, there was only a single wall between them.

'Now my son, what's all this 'ere disturbance?' asked the Prior (himself a Yorkshireman) when at last the drunkard was allowed at his own insistence within the sacred walls.

'Tha sees — *hic*', said Brother Jucundus (as he was to be), 'it's like this — Ah'd very much like to join thy Order, if tha'll nobbut 'ave me. Ah've seen t' error of mi ways, tha sees — all this suppin' an' carryin' on is no

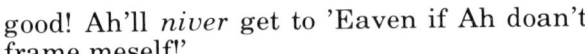

good! Ah'll *niver* get to 'Eaven if Ah doan't frame meself!'

Like most good men, the Prior was something of an optimist. He must have been. Anyone else in medieval York just then could have told him what to expect.

'My son', he said, tears welling in his tired old eyes, 'thou givest me great joy. If only others would learn to see t' folly of their wicked ways as thou hast done and would repent in time, we righteous folk would all be fair chuffed. Welcome to t' Brotherhood, lad!'

He sent for the Novice Master, who took one look at his new pupil and almost handed in his notice on the spot. Almost, I say, because instead, he resolved there and then that though the future Jucundus might have broken a dozen mothers' hearts, he would not break that of the Novice Master of St. Leonard's Priory.

Drunk as he was, I fancy the new brother may have caught the gleam in the Master's eye and asked himself: 'Hast jumped out o' t' secular fryin' pan into t' sacred fire Jucundus, lad?'

Before many days had passed he was convinced that he had! He began to long for his old, carefree drunken days and when York Fair came along in its annual wonted way, the sounds of revelry that filtered through the Priory walls were too great a temptation.

Jucundus watched his opportunity and when the Novice Master was looking the other way, borrowed a small loan from the poor box and slipped through the gate to mingle joyfully with the roistering throng.

Pretty soon he was engaged in some serious drinking. Tankard after tankard he sided. Suddenly, a swingboat ride seemed irresistible to his fuddled mind, and that was to prove his undoing!

For as Brother Jucundus soared skyward, joyfully, singing

In dulce jubilo

Up, up, up we go

who should spot him but the Novice Master and a couple of his henchmonks. 'Ah think', said the Novice Master politely, 'tha's got that wrong, brother. Tha means

down, down, down we come! Forward with thy barrow, Brother Retribution, please.'

They bundled Jucundus into the wheelbarrow and took him back to the Priory, where the Father Prior, with tears in his sad old eyes, gently told Jucundus that he was to be walled up alive in the wine cellar.

'An' tha mustn't think, Juc, lad', said the old man 'that this doesn't 'urt me more —'

'Ah know what you're goin' to say, Dad', Jucundus interrupted, deeply moved, 'an' it's a rare consolation — it is that!' Soon he was walled in and left to his fate . . .

With melancholy mien he eyed the cruse of water and the loaf of bread that was the Father Prior's idea of a picnic lunch for anyone bound for eternity. Perhaps that was what did it. To a man of Jucundus's temperament there was something almost obscene about the sight of that frugal repast. The thought of sitting next to that for ever and ever was suddenly unbearable. In his panic he began to struggle and his considerable bulk was rather more than the old wine cellar walls could contain.

A stone shifted . . . he struggled again. This time he could see daylight between the stones. Cautiously he pushed one out and found himself looking into the neighbouring St. Mary's Abbey!

Jucundus shook his head almost in disbelief. 'If Ah'm not a dab 'and at goin' fra' bad to worse . . .' he said. For he knew that St. Mary's was a Cistercian house and very strict. Even so, its strictness was to prove highly convenient for Jucundus, for one of its rules was silence, which saved the new brother (as he was considered) from having to answer too many embarrassing questions.

Poor Jucundus was far from pleased with his new order. The rule of silence meant that he could not even bolster his spirits with a song. And it hardly cheered him up to know that in just a few days York Fair would be in full swing again outside the abbey walls. So a whole year had passed! It seemed like a century . . .

Then, just as it does in fiction, the unexpected happened: the monk in charge of the wine-cellar died, and the brethren of St. Mary's were so ill-advised as to give the job to Jucundus. They had made the mistake of thinking Jucundus was abstemious, but the truth was that he would not insult his palate with the poor watery ale served at their abbey!

He must surely have felt that his luck had changed at last. Suddenly he no longer felt such a great need to break out and go to the fair. With the whole of the Abbey's wine and beer at his disposal, it seemed as though the fair had come to him! And not a penny to pay . . .

Lying in his cell the night before the fair, he suddenly felt that there was no point in waiting longer. For Brother Jucundus, the fair would start tonight!

Once in the cellar he wasted no time on the lesser brews and vintages. Starting with the malmsey, he worked his way through the most precious wines labelled 'Kings and Archbishops only', then he tackled those reserved for 'Bishops, Sheriffs and Foreign Princelings'. By the time he had reached the shelves marked 'Aldermen and Small Town Mayors', the fine edge of his palate was blunted — and so was his caution.

As always, when he was concentrating, he began to sing.

His brother monks, who got little enough sleep at the best of times, looked less than kindly upon the disturber of their slumbers, and when Jucundus was extricated from the cellar, he found himself once again on a serious charge and facing the Abbot.

The charge was read out; the penalty pronounced — death, of course.

'Ah want thee to know —' began the Abbot.

'Ah do', said Jucundus. 'This hurts thee more than it does me, an' I'm right sluffened about that. Now, Ah wouldn't do this for anybody, but — how dosta feel about swoppin' places? Seein' it upsets thee so much, Ah mean . . .'

'Nay, nay', said the Abbot, 'justice must be done'.
''Ere — *hic* — we go again', said Jucundus.

He was walled up with the regulation cruse of water and a loaf of bread, but this time he was almost too drunk to care. And as usual, when he was fair flummoxed what to do next, he sang, and sang, and sang . . .

And that was why the cellarer at St. Leonard's next door, on his way to fetch the evening beer, dropped his flagon from trembling hands as he recognized the unmistakable voice of the same Brother Jucundus he had helped to entomb alive in that very wall a full year before.

'Brothers, brothers,' cried the cellarer, tumbling back up the steps again, 'a miracle! Come and see . . .'

In minutes they had torn down the wall and dragged Jucundus back into the daylight, marvelling that the bread and water were untouched as they had left them.

It was, of course, just Jucundus's luck that the very Prior of St. Leonard's who had ordered his entombment 12 months before had just died. A successor was as yet still to be found, but could there be a plainer sign of heaven's intentions than this amazing discovery? Jucundus had returned to St. Leonard's by means of a miracle that would turn their habits permanently green with envy next door at St. Mary's.

'Ah don't mind if Ah do, lads,' he said modestly, when asked if he would take the job. 'At least Ah'll make sure you get some decent ale to sup!'

Comical Capital

If Yorkshire has a comic capital it is surely Holmfirth! Not only did it anticipate Hollywood by making slapstick comedies in which the local population played all the parts, it is also one of the biggest comic postcard producers in the world.

Latterly television has discovered Holmfirth and tried to impose its own ideas of comedy on this moorland

setting. Whether or not it has succeeded must be a matter of taste, but of one thing I'm certain: the actors and producers who screen such programmes as 'Last of the Summer Wine' never enjoyed their work half as much as did the locals who produced their home-made epics from 1899 or thereabouts.

Realism was all in those days. And when the producer wanted an exciting fight to take place in a boat on the lake in Honley Pleasure Gardens, three miles away, he knew exactly how to get just the right effect.

First — a private word with each of his stars in turn — Freddie Bullock and Fred Beaumont (who, because he was a french polisher by trade, rejoiced in the nickname 'Shiner').

Immaculate in frock coats and top hats the two set sail upon the lake. Then, at a signal from the producer — or whoever occupied the chair of power in those days — the fun began ... for the spectators, that is. Each man jumped to his feet and tried with frustrated might and main to push his companion into the lake.

Result: stalemate.'*Will yer — get out o' t' — boat?*' demanded Freddie, between shoves.

'*Nay*', Shiner replied, in the pauses between his own exertions, 'it's *me* — who 'as to push *thee* — out o' t' boat'.

'Tha's — got it — all — wrong', retorted Freddie, now virtually apoplectic. 'E said *I* 'ad to push *thee* out. Give up *pushin*' yer fool! Yer'll 'ave us both in t' watter!'

Meanwhile, the cameras rolled and the film-maker, whoever he was, could hardly crank his camera for rubbing his hands with joy at the marvellously convincing action — and all without a single rehearsal. Inevitably, just as the producer had planned, both his stars ended up in the lake.

When he was not acting for the cameras, Shiner was sometimes to be found polishing coffins in the taproom of the Jolly Hatter. Once he hid himself in a coffin, and whilst an unsuspecting customer was drinking at the bar, he slowly raised the lid and accompanied its creaking with a sepulchral, shivering groan: 'Aw I am cowd! *Aw*, I am co-o-wd!'

Very few such performances were needed before the customer staggered to another pub across the road. 'Coom to t' Jolly 'Atter', he earnestly exhorted the clientele, '*hic* — they're burying' the buggers wick theer!'

Shiner was undoubtedly a gift to any producer of comic films, but his roles were not without peril, for in those days stars had no stand-ins.

Once he and Freddie were 'signed up' to portray two villains locked in the village stocks and being pelted with fruit by the villagers.

No doubt during the pelting Freddie regretted the fact that when buying the fruit he had not confined himself to the softer varieties, because pretty soon the crowd's enthusiasm ran away with them.

Both Shiner and Freddie were taking a terrible hammering, and when someone at last decided to release them from the stocks for safety's sake, the two comedians had to run for their lives. I hope they saw the funny side of that!

Tragedy was narrowly averted on another occasion when a local 'fat lady' weighing all of 22 stones found herself stuck in the window of the 'burning house' where she was meant to cut a dramatic filmic figure. Fortunately, her colleagues realized that her agitated cries for help were rather more than mere overacting and she was rescued. The film-making ended in 1914 when, incidentally, an order from Russia for a hundred films was cancelled.

It had all begun when James Bamforth, the son of a Holmfirth painter and decorator, turned his talents to wet plate photography.

Those were the days of lantern lectures, and James painted the backcloths in front of which living models posed for the photographer amid artificial scenery. He began illustrating books by this method, one of the most successful being Silas Hocking's *Her Benny*.

Then in 1890 James found an additional outlet — cards illustrating popular songs and hymns.

They not only provided Holmfirth with a kind of village industry to supplement the staple of worsted manufacture, they allowed worthy citizens to lead what was virtually a double life! And all without losing a jot of respect — if leaving a somewhat puzzling legacy to their families!

Take Herbert Battye, a tailor of repute, several times council chairman, vicar's warden for years at Holmfirth Parish Church . . . and goodness knows *what* else in his spare time while he was posing for the cameraman engaged on Bamforth's 'Song and Hymn' series!

Let Kathleen M. Battye, who told Herbert's story in *Yorkshire Life,* tell it here . . . 'I never really knew my father-in-law, Herbert Battye, not personally that is. He died thirteen years before I met and married his son. But I feel that he somehow is no stranger to me, although I must say that at first I found his personality baffling.

'What, I ask you, is a diffident daughter-in-law, anxious to please her husband's family and win their approval, to make of a parent-in-law who could sometimes be seen in a rustic setting, gazing tenderly at a winsome country lass, or by the fireside, murmuring endearments to a demure miss who had just finished presiding over the tea table?

'At other times he would be found, suave and worldly in a black coat and silk hat, talking persuasively to a simple country girl, or in sober Sunday best, standing at the altar with his bride. He could even be espied — shame on him — dead drunk on the public house floor, or in sailor's uniform on the quay dejectedly contemplating what seemed to be a kit bag containing all his possessions. Hardly surprising that he should be leaving home, really, with his private life in such a tangle!

'It wasn't as if his family didn't try to help. His sister met him once outside the saloon bar, and pleaded with him not to go in. It was much too late for such concern — he was already swaying in the doorway of the King's Arms, crumpled and unkempt, doggedly determined to enter, whatever the cost.

'His sainted elderly mother, a lady fond of biblical wall texts, sent for him and lectured him on his dissolute ways, but all to no avail! His life continued in much the same way, an odd blend of depravity and respectability . . .

'None of his friends and associates ever reproached him for leading such a scandalous double life, which wasn't very surprising, for they were all busily engaged in doing precisely the same thing themselves . . .'

Talk about making your own amusement!

A card illustrating the song *Goodbye Dolly Gray* was a best-seller during the South African conflict. In the Great War which followed, the blend of sentimentality and patriotism was even more successful. Bamforth's were shrewd enough to print one stanza on each numbered card, so that if you wanted to send your dear boy at the Front *all* the words of *There's a long long trail* or *When the fields are white with daisies* (suitably illustrated with heroic soldiers and sailors and their pensive sweethearts) you had to buy three or four cards.

'Sentimentality Holmfirth' might have been an appropriate telegraphic address for Bamforth's in those days, but in the desolate years following the War to End Wars, sentiment took rather a beating and the firm found themselves with huge stocks of the old cards left on their hands.

Bamforth's might indeed have perished along with sentiment had they not been able to turn a quip as readily as they had jerked a tear. Comedy cards now became the order of the day, though you'd have to be very ticklish to get an easy laugh from some of them today!

A photographic card produced in 1909 shows a mildly chaotic skating rink scene and bears the caption, 'This is what I call lively'. Well, to each his own . . . Perhaps the few inches of bloomered leg displayed by some of the 'fallen women' among the skaters was the 'lively' bit, but to my mind a *bona fide* notice insisting that 'Gentlemen must skate with Hats removed' is at least as funny.

Other early cards showed that henpecked husbands were as fair game then as now. 'My wife's joined the Suffrage Movement' (says one poor, aproned soul as he polishes the brass fender). 'I've suffered ever since!'

Cards reflect the age producing them. Besides the perennial fat women, henpecked husbands and honeymoon couples, I remember — from Blackpool holidays in the '30s — a plethora of impossibly foaming tankards usually accompanied by huge plates of fish and chips. The idea was, presumably, that the northerner on holiday would send these home in the certain knowledge that they would reduce his work-bound colleagues to frenzied envy.

In these better-fed days, the fish and chips are perhaps less noticeable. So what is the constant factor in comic cardology? Years ago, the grandson of the James Bamforth who founded the Holmfirth empire told me that the great card-seller was undoubtedly vulgarity. But 'we never publish anything obscene'.

In those days Bamforth's sent every new design produced in their moorland studio to a censorship committee at Blackpool whose members included a clergyman, a solicitor, a barrister, members of various women's organizations and representatives of the wholesale and retail trades.

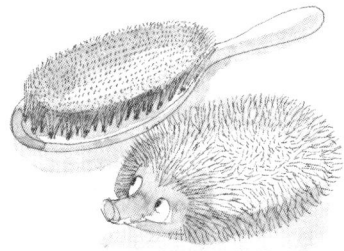

'Anything they turn down we destroy', Derek Bamforth explained without apparent regret. Though not, one felt, without an occasional sense of puzzlement.

For instance, a well developed bust could properly be confused with a 'nice juicy pear' but a harmless hedgehog casting doubtful glances at a hairbrush over the caption 'Mixed marriages don't work' was rejected. At first sight it wasn't easy to see why.

Also rejected on that occasion was a card showing the perennial couple in bed with this accompanying dialogue — 'Wife: Why don't you bite my ear in bed like you used to. Husband: I can't. My teeth are in the bathroom.'

Another rejection: 'I see he has his mother's rosy cheeks', says a visitor to a blushing young mother whose offspring lies, as nature made him, face down across her knee. Another: 'You've got stomach trouble', says a doctor to his patient. 'You'll have to diet'. Patient: 'What colour?'

Were the Blackpool Committee being over-fussy in remembering that many people are sensitive about subjects like mixed marriages, false teeth and stomach trouble? After all, humour itself would die if the 'someone-won't-like-this rule' were universally and strictly enforced.

I now consider myself enough of an expert to be able to

spot a Bamforth card on sight. For one thing they are better drawn and printed than many, and the jokes are funnier. Most noticeable of all, they are inspired by a joy in living, which is painfully absent from many cards put out by other firms, some of which can only be described as childishly nasty.

Bamforth bosoms may be overdeveloped, but the girls who display them are often delightfully pretty, whereas the girls depicted in some rival productions look as if they were drawn by embittered misogynists.

I wondered what James Bamforth, who looked down from the wall in Victorian dignity, would think of the firm he founded and the cards they are producing now.

Would he be amused by the termagant wife who tells her bed-ridden husband, 'You're having no more whisky — there'll be none left for the funeral!'? Or by the voyeur window cleaner saying to the girl in her bath, 'Your phone's ringing, Miss. Why don't you answer it?' Or by the boy and girl tots peering down into their pyjamas and saying *Vive la difference*?

I rather think he would — but tastes in humour change. Like one of Bamforth's charmers, who doesn't know that her bottom is showing in the mirror behind her, he might simply demand, 'What the devil are *you* laughing at?'

An example of a 'spicier' Bamforth comic of today.

The Infernal Triangle

I met him at the National Brass Band championships. There, I said to myself as I watched him leaning morosely on the bar of the Drum and Trumpet, a little known hostelry in the neighbourhood of the Albert Hall, there leans a man with a Secret Sorrow.

I bought him a pint and his sorrow did not stay secret for long . . .

'Did you see yond drummer in t' Brighouse an' Rastrick?' he asked with wistful eagerness, 'Ah came all t' way from Luddendenfoot just to watch him. Mind you, Black Dyke drummer was nearly as good!'

'There were some splendid musicians in every band', I murmured soothingly.

'But t'*drummers* — t' drummers is best', he insisted, a wild gleam in his eye. 'T' drummers is best,' he repeated, his words tailing away and ending almost in a sob.

What, I wondered, was the reason for this strange fixation about drums? Foolishly I tried to cure him of it.

'Surely', I said, 'you would agree that the trombones were magnificent in *March of the Tripe and Onions*. After all, every instrument has its part to play. In *Black Pudding Polka* even the humble triangle —'

He startled me by giving almost a shriek of horror — '*The triangle* — don't mention *the triangle*. An' don't ask me to tell you the 'ole agonising story, I beg of yer. Don't ask — *please!*'

'Of course not', I said, reassuringly.

'But I expect Ah shall 'ave to', he replied, staring morosely into his empty glass.

'Another pint, please', I said. And this is the tale he told . . .

'Ah was never allowed to play the drum in t' percussion band at school; always they fobbed me off with the triangle. And this deprivation has left an ineradicable mark on my psyche — or summat.

'Ah *desperately* longed to play the drum. I could *see* myself with it. Ah felt it was *me*. Triangle was *not* me, and t' fact that anybody could think otherwise was an 'umiliation from which Ah've still not recovered to this day.

'Our school percussion band, to t' best of my recollection, knew only one tune — *In an English Country Garden*. We each had us own bits to play, accompanied by Miss 'Owthwaite on t' piano, and the final result (which must have been educational — 'cos it certainly wasn't musical) went summat like —
    Bang-tiddly-bok-bok bangti-bangti-clang
    In an English country BANG-ti
    ping!

'That ping — at t' end — was *me*, tha sees, with mi triangle. Sad to say, Ah was a bit given to mind-wandering even then, and sometimes Ah must admit mi ping came a bit late. Sometimes Ah missed it altogether, and terrible then was the wrath of Miss 'Owthwaite! Ah quickly learned the 'ard way that while English country gardens might end on a ping, they *never,* they simply *couldn't* just end on a bang-ti!

'As t' days passed I became more and more desperate to play the drum, Ah joined the Wolf Cubs, only to find that they didn't play drums until they'd 'atched into Scouts. Could I, I asked miself, wait that long? No, I answered miself, Ah couldn't. Ah seconded myself to t'Boys' Brigade who had an even noisier band than the Scouts, but with no better luck. Because early on t' first Sunday after I'd joined, a maddened willeyer on t' night shift, unable to face another band practice, broke into t' H.Q. and wreaked such 'avoc with a ten-inch nail that not a drumskin was left intact. Not a solitary skin . . .

'And so it went on — frustration after frustration, and after I'd been turned down by t'bandmaster of the local Territorials (who bore an uncanny resemblance to Miss 'Owthwaite) I almost lost hope.

'The iron — as they say — finally entered mi soul after mi application to become t' big drummer were rejected by t' Salvation Army. With a certain lack of Christian charity, Ah might add!

'"And now we'll sing *Tell me the old, old story'*, said Captain Pennyfeather (a most unmusical man, I allus felt), after t' final refusal.

'Don't bother, Ah've heard it, Ah said, and Ah tossed his tambourine right back at him. Under t' stress of emotion, mi aim was 'appen a bit wide, and t' daft instrument lodged briefly between the jaws of a large

Songster . . . She'd ta'en a bit o' shuttin' up, but that did it!

'*Don't* think I haven't tried to cure miself of this obsession.

'Ah've looked for it in books on psychiatry, only to find that the condition has been ignored — completely ignored. Not a single entry could I find under Drum (deprivation of) or Percussion paranoia. Not a bloody one!

'When Ah became a man, Ah should have put away childish things, Ah know that, but any resemblance between St. Paul and me is, alas, purely 'allucinatory.

'Ah got married. Hopefully and in due course Ah bought mi little lad a drum, but after Ah'd beaten it — ecstatic like — for one delirious afternoon it disappeared and I found t' little chap screwing a padlock to t' toy cupboard door.

'Time passed, like it does, an' that boy eventually became a teenager. I don't hold it against him: I'm sure he'd 'ave avoided it if he could. But, being a teenager, he had to belong to A Group. They 'ad some sort of name . . . The Dregs, The Creeps or summat — and they were as oddly assorted a bunch as you'd care to meet. I never cared to — meet them, Ah mean — but Ah was irresistibly drawn by the magnificent drum kit possessed by one of 'em, a little 'orror known as Sweep. (I was never sure why — must have had summat to do with t' colour of his neck.)'

He looked up at me pathetically. 'What was Ah sayin'?' he demanded vaguely. 'Ah've dried up!'

'The Group', I prompted, gently. 'Who else was in the Group? . . . Another pint here, please'.

'Oh aye, the Group. There was another of 'em called The Prof, a gangling, bespectacled youth with the air of a demented Lancashire giraffe, much given to inventing things when he wasn't actually *wailing* into t' microphone like a dyspeptic banshee — he Did the Vocals, I gathered, an' that came as rather a surprise, because I'd been under t' impression he made that noise with one of 'is own inventions, 'idden in 'is teeth.

"'Look, Daddyo', said my son one day as I came upon t' Group practising in t' garage. "I wish you wouldn't — like — *snoop around* when we're practising. It's distracting, man, distracting!"

'I cast an appealing glance at Sweep's drum kit. "Couldn't I just —"

"'Beat it, Daddyo", said Sweep. "And I don't mean the drum! This is a real all-gone-out-type group with which you strictly do not cohere."

"'He means, 'Go'," my son explained. 'I felt like a Red Indian denied his firewatter. "Group speak with forked tongue", I said, "but I get message. Someday you be sorry, maybe".

'I turned on mi 'eel and strode proudly back to t' family wigwam.

'Sure enough that day came — for them to be sorry, Ah mean. The Dregs, desperate for wealth and fame, accepted a booking at our local Working Men's Club, and it was from there my son rang me up . . . An' 'is voice were *strangely 'umbled!*

"'Dad," he said. "You remember asking if you could play in the Group? Well, you can. Tonight at least. Sweep's been taken right poorly."

"'The Black Death?" I enquired, all icy-like, concealing mi excitement. "Oh well, I don't mind helping you out. Be there in ten minutes."

'Secretly, of course, the thought of having Sweep's drum kit all to miself for a 'ole evening, and with an audience, thrown in, was enough to send me fair delirious with joy. But that joy was short-lived!

"'What, *you* on the drums?" said mi son an' heir when I got there — an' he bust out laughin'. "Oh, no, Daddyo, that's not the idea at all. *I'm* going to play the drums. You're going to play a new instrument the Prof's just invented. It's a sort of steel circle like, an' you 'it it with a steel rod and it makes a way-out pinging sound. *Crazy, man!*"

"'Oh, no!" I groaned. How could fate be so cruel? It was mi old enemy the triangle. Only round, man, round!

"'We're starting with *On Ilkla' Moor Baht Hang-ups.* One, two, a *one*-two-three-four —"

"'Hod on a minute", Ah said, "I don't think I know that one".

"'Oh, well, play what you know!"

'And so,' concluded my friend, accepting a third pint, 'not only the triangle but the wheel of fate itself came full circle! And while t' Creeps gave out with *On Ilkla' Moor*, etc., I could nobbut manage

In an English Country Ga-ar-
                PING!'

But don't you *dare* laugh at Heckmondwike!

> It has a 'Green' as black as ink,
> It has a river called 'The Stink',
> And much to cause a man to think;
> In Heckmondwike.
>
> *Clock Almanack 1907*

Heckmondwike, they tell me, means *place-of-refuge-in-the-forest-fortified-with-an-earthwork-enclosure*. But if I could get away with it, I might tell you it meant *place-where-they-thought-of-it-first*.

It had illuminations before Blackpool, and a public fire brigade before London. Joseph Priestley, the discoverer of oxygen, lived in Heckmondwike for twenty years and John Curwen, inventor of Tonic Solfa, was born there. A few years ago a Heckmondwike carpet mill achieved another first by producing a kind of carpet for ski-ing without snow. Whativver next! And even now I've mentioned only a few of the pioneers.

To judge indeed by the town's successes you might almost conclude that God, if not a Heckmondwike chap, must be a Nonconformist. And appropriately, the opening of the first Upper Independent Chapel in 1701 stands out in Heckmondwike's annals. For t' Upper was no ordinary chapel. If its adherents had any doubts of the Almighty's special favour and protection, these must have been quelled for ever after one rather Old Testament incident.

Apparently the congregation were anxious to extend the chapel into a field at the rear, but the owner of the land refused to sell. Even the few yards which were available were intruded upon by a branch of a giant oak growing on the owner's land.

Prayer meetings were called and the Lord was entreated to 'soften the stubborn heart of the owner of the tree'. There is no record that this was achieved — perhaps they were asking too much! Anyway, the Lord had more drastic methods at his disposal, and during the night following one of these prayer meetings, the tree was struck by lightning and 'shattered into a thousand fragments.'

The present huge Upper Chapel — 'all t' others is pups off this one', I was told — is the fourth to be built on this site. Its graveyard contains impressive tombstones to the illustrious dissenting dead of a bygone age — with names like Wharton, Firth, Rhodes and Morton — families which made Heckmondwike the rich little town it became. On Lecture Days their carriages and pairs lined Chapel Lane.

Lecture Days? Yes. 'T' Lectures', dating from 1761, can fairly be said to be among Heckmondwike's claims to fame — a survival from the 1750s when an academy was formed at nearby Norristhorpe to train students for the ministry.

Outstanding preachers are still* to be heard at the Lectures, but these occasions are neither so fashionable nor so snobbish as in the days when, a septuagenarian told me, he took his latest girl friend to hear the famous evangelist Gypsy Smith. The couple inadvertently sat in a pew belonging to a wealthy family of the day and were promptly evicted!

Not the sort of event to which a modern young man might take his girl, perhaps, but those lectures were considered swinging events in bygone Heckmondwike, more of a festive occasion, even, than Christmas. They produced their own special dish, Lecture Pudding, which could be seen hanging from kitchen ceilings in preparation for the great day when perhaps twenty relations would turn up for Lecture Dinner, for which a whole hind-quarter of lamb had been bought.

Whatever their other shortcomings, in those days they were not afraid of originality: they were nonconformist in more than religion, with characters like William ('Boy') Preston, the bearded Town Crier; Johnny Lonkey, the scissor grinder, and 'Lord Kettlewell'.

Johnny Lonkey, reputed to have served as a cabin boy in the ship which took Napoleon to St. Helena, once undertook to walk 1,000 miles in 1,000 consecutive hours trundling his scissor machine. A track was prepared and a committee appointed to check the results. Lonkey made good his boast and swore that he could have gone on for another hundred miles. Apparently his family kept him well fortified on his marathon by means of a teapot which did not contain tea.

* Alas, the last Lecture was the last indeed — *sic transit gloria Heckmondwike.*

Then there was Sammy Senior, the very popular local preacher, much sought after for anniversary services, One chapel, having fallen on rather hard times, sent a deputation to see Sammy in the hope of getting his services at a reduced rate.

'Let's see,' said Sammy, 'Ah came for ten shillin' t' last time. Well, Ah could come for seven an' six, an' Ah could come for five shillin', but it 'ud be poor stuff for seven an' six, an' it wouldn't be worth listenin' to for five shillin'.' He got his ten bob.

From the outbreak of war until 1950, Heckmondwike dimmed its famous illuminations. At the Christmases of today they shine again, and if proof were needed of the town's faith in itself, the 'Lights' would provide it. Costing £53 (a considerable sum) in 1885 when they first flickered, they demonstrate still that hard-headedness and imagination *can* go hand in hand.

Today, reluctantly, I dare say, the town is part of a bigger authority, but the spirit which made the place, with its Upper Chapel, its mills and its illuminations, will surely survive. After all, you can never really *lose* a name like Heckmondwike...

Other Whitethorn Press publications include:

Queer Folk
A comicality of Yorkshire characters
by Maurice Colbeck
(author of Yorkshire Laughter)
£1.60

Steam-up in Lancashire
Railwayana from 'Lancashire Life'
£1.00

Flower Arrangement — Free Style
by
Edith Brack
£2.20

Just Sithabod
55 dialect poems from 'Lancashire Life'
£1.50

Cheyp at t'Price
More dialect verse from 'Lancashire Life'
£1.50